Preface

Welcome to the **"Cisco Certified Network Associate (CCNA) Interview Questions & Answer"** your essential companion to success in the Cisco Certified Network Associate (CCNA) interviews. Designed with a comprehensive approach, this book serves as a valuable resource to help you navigate the intricate world of networking and emerge confidently in the interview room.

It is with great pleasure that I introduce you to the "CCNA Interview Book," a comprehensive guide meticulously curated to elevate your preparation for Cisco Certified Network Associate (CCNA) interviews. In today's dynamic technology landscape, networking professionals are in high demand, and securing a CCNA certification is a crucial step toward a rewarding career. This book is crafted to not only assist you in mastering the intricacies of CCNA but also to excel in the interview process that follows.

As you embark on this journey, you will find an extensive collection of interview s that delve into various aspects of networking—ranging from fundamental concepts to advanced protocols. Each is designed not just to test your knowledge but to provide you with an opportunity to showcase your expertise in a real-world context. The answers provided are not mere solutions; they are comprehensive explanations aimed at deepening your understanding and preparing you for the diverse challenges that networking roles often present.

Whether you are a seasoned professional aiming for career advancement or a dedicated learner on the cusp of entering the networking domain, this book caters to your specific needs. From subnetting and routing to security and troubleshooting, we cover it all to ensure a well-rounded preparation for your CCNA interviews.

Table of Contents

Chapter 1: Interview Questions & AnswersPart 1

Q.1 What is the purpose of a MAC address?

Answer: A MAC (Media Access Control) address is a unique identifier assigned to a network interface card (NIC) to facilitate communication within a network. It operates at the data link layer of the OSI model.

Q.2Differentiate between a hub and a switch.

Answer: A hub operates at the physical layer, broadcasting data to all devices in a network, causing collisions. In contrast, a switch operates at the data link layer, forwarding data only to the specific device it is intended for, reducing collisions and improving network efficiency.

Q.3 Explain the concept of an IP address.

Answer: An IP (Internet Protocol) address is a numerical label assigned to each device on a network to facilitate communication. It is composed of two parts: the network portion and the host portion, providing a hierarchical structure for routing.

Q.4What is the purpose of a subnet mask?

Answer: A subnet mask is used to divide an IP address into network and host portions. It helps in organizing and managing IP addresses efficiently within a network, allowing for better control of routing and addressing.

Q.5 Describe the role of a router in a network.

Answer: A router operates at the network layer and is responsible for forwarding data between different networks. It uses routing tables to determine the best path for data transmission, connecting disparate networks and facilitating inter-network communication.

Q.6 What is the significance of the OSI model in networking?

Answer: The OSI (Open Systems Interconnection) model is a conceptual framework with seven layers, each handling specific tasks in network communication. It provides a standardized approach, aiding in the understanding, design, and troubleshooting of network interactions.

Q.7 Explain the difference between TCP and UDP.

Answer: TCP (Transmission Control Protocol) provides reliable, connection-oriented communication with error checking, while UDP (User Datagram Protocol) is connectionless and faster, suitable for applications where occasional data loss is acceptable.

Q.8 What is a default gateway?

Answer: A default gateway is the IP address of a router used when a device needs to communicate with a device on another network. It serves as the entry and exit point for traffic leaving or entering a network.

Q.9 How does DNS (Domain Name System) work?

Answer: DNS translates human-readable domain names into IP addresses, facilitating easy navigation on the internet. It operates as a distributed hierarchical database, converting domain names to corresponding IP addresses.

Q.10 What role does a firewall play in network security?

Answer: A firewall is a network security device that monitors and controls incoming and outgoing network traffic based on predetermined security rules. It acts as a barrier between a trusted internal network and untrusted external networks, enhancing overall network security.

Q.11What is the OSI model, and why is it important in networking?

Answer: The OSI (Open Systems Interconnection) model is a conceptual framework with seven layers, defining the functions of a telecommunication or computing system. It's crucial in networking for providing a standardized approach to understanding, designing, and troubleshooting network interactions.

Q.12 Briefly explain each layer of the OSI model.

Answer: The OSI model consists of seven layers: Physical, Data Link, Network, Transport, Session, Presentation, and Application. Each layer has specific responsibilities, such as dealing with physical connectivity, addressing, routing, and user interfaces.

Q.13 How does the OSI model aid in network troubleshooting?

Answer: The OSI model provides a layered approach, allowing network administrators to isolate and troubleshoot issues at a specific layer. This systematic approach simplifies the identification of problems and speeds up the resolution process.

Q.14 Why is the OSI model often compared to a "stack"?

Answer: The OSI model is often referred to as a stack because the layers build upon one another, with each layer relying on the services provided by the layer below it. This hierarchical structure helps in understanding the flow of data through a network.

Q.15 How does the Transport layer differ from the Network layer in the OSI model?

Answer: The Transport layer is responsible for end-to-end communication and error recovery, often using protocols like TCP or UDP. The Network layer, on the other hand, handles logical addressing, routing, and forwarding of data between different networks.

Q.16 Explain the function of the Presentation layer.

Answer: The Presentation layer is responsible for translating data between the Application layer and the lower layers. It manages data formats, encryption, and compression, ensuring that data is presented in a readable format for the Application layer.

Q.17 Why is the OSI model considered a "reference model"?

Answer: The OSI model is a reference model because it provides a conceptual framework that guides the development of networking standards. It does not prescribe specific technologies but serves as a reference for understanding and creating network protocols.

Q.18 How does the Data Link layer handle error detection?

Answer: The Data Link layer is responsible for framing data into frames and detecting errors using techniques like Cyclic Redundancy Check (CRC). It ensures data integrity within the same network segment.

Q.19 In what way does the Application layer interact with end-user processes?

Answer: The Application layer provides network services directly to end-user applications. It handles communication functions such as file transfers, email, and database queries, ensuring seamless interaction with user processes.

Q.20 Can you provide an example of a protocol associated with each layer of the OSI model?

Answer: Certainly! Examples include Ethernet (Data Link), IP (Network), TCP/UDP (Transport), HTTP (Application), and others. Associating protocols with each layer aids in understanding the functionalities at each level of the OSI model.

Q.21 What is TCP/IP, and why is it important in networking?

Answer: TCP/IP (Transmission Control Protocol/Internet Protocol) is the foundational suite of protocols for the internet. It facilitates communication between devices on a network, providing a standardized framework for data transmission and addressing.

Q.22 Differentiate between TCP and IP.

Answer: TCP (Transmission Control Protocol) is responsible for reliable, connection-oriented communication, ensuring data delivery without errors. IP (Internet Protocol) is responsible for logical addressing and routing, determining how data packets should be forwarded across networks.

Q.23 Explain the role of an IP address in the TCP/IP protocol suite.

Answer: An IP address uniquely identifies a device on a network. It allows for the proper routing and delivery of data packets to the intended recipient, serving as a critical component in the TCP/IP addressing scheme.

Q.24 What is the purpose of subnetting in TCP/IP networking?

Answer: Subnetting is used to divide a large IP network into smaller, more manageable sub-networks. It enhances network efficiency, reduces congestion, and facilitates better IP address management.

Q.25 How does DHCP (Dynamic Host Configuration Protocol) work in TCP/IP networks?

Answer: DHCP dynamically assigns IP addresses to devices on a network, eliminating the need for manual configuration. It operates at the Application layer of the TCP/IP model, simplifying the management of IP addresses in large networks.

Q.26 Describe the process of DNS (Domain Name System) resolution.

Answer: DNS translates human-readable domain names into IP addresses. When a user enters a domain name, DNS resolves it to the corresponding IP address, facilitating seamless communication on the internet.

Q.27 What is the purpose of the TCP three-way handshake?

Answer: The TCP three-way handshake establishes a reliable connection between two devices. It involves the exchange of SYN and ACK flags, confirming the readiness for data transfer and ensuring synchronization between sender and receiver.

Q.28 How does NAT (Network Address Translation) contribute to TCP/IP networking?

Answer: NAT allows multiple devices in a private network to share a single public IP address when accessing the internet. It enhances security and conserves public IP addresses by mapping private addresses to a single public address.

Q.29 Explain the function of the ARP (Address Resolution Protocol) in TCP/IP networks.

Answer: ARP is used to map a known IP address to a MAC (Media Access Control) address within a local network. It ensures proper communication by associating IP addresses with their corresponding hardware addresses.

Q.30 What is ICMP (Internet Control Message Protocol) used for in the TCP/IP suite?

Answer: ICMP is a network layer protocol that facilitates communication between network devices by reporting errors and providing diagnostic information. It is commonly used for tools like Ping and Traceroute to troubleshoot network connectivity issues.

Q.31 What is Ethernet, and how does it function in local area networks (LANs)?

Answer: Ethernet is a widely used LAN technology that employs a bus or star topology. It uses a contention-based access method called Carrier Sense Multiple Access with Collision Detection (CSMA/CD) to manage data collisions and ensure efficient communication within a LAN.

Q.32 Differentiate between half-duplex and full-duplex communication in Ethernet.

Answer: In half-duplex, devices can either send or receive data at any given time, while in full-duplex, devices can simultaneously send and receive data. Ethernet can operate in both half-duplex (CSMA/CD) and full-duplex modes.

Q.33 What is a MAC address, and how is it used in Ethernet?

Answer: A MAC (Media Access Control) address is a unique identifier assigned to a network interface card (NIC). In Ethernet, the MAC address is used for frame delivery, helping devices on a network communicate by addressing frames to specific hardware addresses.

Q.34 Explain the concept of VLAN (Virtual Local Area Network).

Answer: A VLAN is a logical grouping of devices in a network, even if they are not physically connected on the same switch. VLANs help in enhancing network security, reducing broadcast traffic, and simplifying network management.

Q.35 What is the purpose of a switch in Ethernet networks?

Answer: A switch operates at the data link layer of the OSI model and is used to connect devices within the same LAN. Unlike hubs, switches forward data only to the specific device it is intended for, reducing collisions and improving network efficiency.

Q.36 How does Spanning Tree Protocol (STP) contribute to Ethernet networks?

Answer: STP prevents loops in Ethernet networks by selectively blocking redundant paths, ensuring a loop-free topology. This prevents broadcast storms and improves the stability of the network.

Q.37 What is the role of ARP (Address Resolution Protocol) in Ethernet communication?

Answer: ARP is used to map IP addresses to MAC addresses within a local network. When a device needs to communicate with another device on the same subnet, ARP resolves the destination IP address to the corresponding MAC address.

Q.38 Explain the difference between a hub and a switch in Ethernet networks.

Answer: A hub operates at the physical layer, broadcasting data to all devices on a network, causing collisions. In contrast, a switch operates at the data link layer, forwarding data only to the specific device it is intended for, reducing collisions and improving network efficiency.

Q.39 What is the significance of Ethernet frame encapsulation?

Answer: Ethernet frame encapsulation is the process of adding header and trailer information to data to form a complete frame. This information includes source and destination MAC addresses, length, and a frame check sequence. It is essential for proper data transmission and reception in Ethernet networks.

Q.40 How does Quality of Service (QoS) play a role in Ethernet networks?

Answer: QoS allows prioritization of network traffic, ensuring that critical data gets precedence over less time-sensitive data. It is crucial in scenarios where bandwidth needs to be allocated efficiently, such as in voice and video communication over Ethernet.

Q.41What is the primary advantage of wireless networking over wired networks?

Answer: The primary advantage of wireless networking is the flexibility and mobility it offers. Users can connect to the network without the constraints of physical cables, enabling increased mobility and convenience.

Q.42 Explain the basic concept of radio frequency (RF) in wireless communication.

Answer: Radio frequency is a range of electromagnetic waves used for wireless communication. In wireless networking, devices communicate using RF signals, and these signals are transmitted and received by antennas.

Q.43 What is SSID, and why is it important in wireless networks?

Answer: SSID (Service Set Identifier) is a unique identifier that distinguishes one wireless network from another. It is essential for wireless devices to connect to the correct network and is often used to enhance network security.

Q.44 How does WEP (Wired Equivalent Privacy) contribute to wireless security?

Answer: WEP is an early wireless security protocol that encrypts data transmitted between wireless devices and the access point. However, it has vulnerabilities and is now largely replaced by more secure protocols like WPA and WPA2.

Q.45 Explain the concept of wireless channels and why channel selection is important.

Answer: Wireless channels are specific frequencies within the RF spectrum. Channel selection is crucial to avoid interference and congestion. Proper channel planning enhances the overall performance of a wireless network.

Q.46 What is the role of a wireless router in a home or office network?

Answer: A wireless router connects wired and wireless devices to a network and facilitates communication between them. It typically includes a built-in switch, DHCP server, and the ability to provide wireless access through Wi-Fi.

Q.47 Describe the difference between 2.4 GHz and 5 GHz frequency bands in wireless networking.

Answer: Both 2.4 GHz and 5 GHz are frequency bands used in wireless networking. The 2.4 GHz band has a longer range but is more prone to interference, while the 5 GHz band offers higher data rates but has a shorter range.

Q.48 What is the purpose of MAC filtering in wireless security?

Answer: MAC filtering allows or denies access to a wireless network based on the MAC addresses of devices. While it provides an additional layer of security, it should be complemented with other security measures for comprehensive protection.

Q.49 How does WPA (Wi-Fi Protected Access) enhance wireless security?

Answer: WPA is a more robust wireless security protocol than WEP. It uses stronger encryption and introduces features like TKIP (Temporal Key Integrity Protocol) and later versions use AES (Advanced Encryption Standard) to secure wireless communication.

Q.50 What is the significance of Wireless Standards like 802.11n and 802.11ac?

Answer: Wireless standards define the specifications for wireless communication. For example, 802.11n and 802.11ac provide faster data rates and improved performance. Understanding these standards is crucial for deploying efficient and compatible wireless networks.

Chapter 2: Interview Questions & Answers Part 2

Q.51 What is the primary function of a router in a network?
Answer: A router is a network device that forwards data packets between different networks. It operates at the network layer (Layer 3) of the OSI model and uses routing tables to determine the best path for data transmission.

Q.52 Explain the difference between a router and a switch.
Answer: A router connects different networks and makes decisions based on logical addressing (IP addresses). A switch operates within a single network and uses MAC addresses to forward frames within that network.

Q.53What is the purpose of a default gateway on a router?
Answer: The default gateway on a router is the IP address used when a device needs to communicate with a device on another network. It serves as the entry and exit point for traffic leaving or entering a network.

Q.54How does NAT (Network Address Translation) work on a router?
Answer: NAT allows multiple devices in a private network to share a single public IP address when accessing the internet. It translates private IP addresses to a single public IP, enhancing security and conserving public IP addresses.

Q.55What is the significance of the router's configuration mode?
Answer: Configuration mode on a router allows network administrators to make changes to the router's settings. It is where commands are entered to define interfaces, set IP addresses, configure routing protocols, and more.

Q.56Explain the purpose of static routing and dynamic routing on a router.
Answer: Static routing involves manually configuring routes on a router, specifying the path that data should take. Dynamic routing uses routing protocols like RIP, OSPF, or EIGRP to automatically update and share routing information between routers.

Q.57How do you secure access to a router's command-line interface (CLI)?
Answer: Access to a router's CLI can be secured using methods like setting passwords, enabling SSH (Secure Shell), and configuring access control lists (ACLs) to restrict who can access the router remotely.

Q.58Describe the process of configuring an IP address on a router interface.
Answer: To configure an IP address on a router interface, you enter the router's configuration mode, navigate to the interface, and use the "ip address" command followed by the desired IP address and subnet mask.

Q.59What is the purpose of router interfaces?

Answer: Router interfaces connect the router to different networks. Each interface typically corresponds to a specific network segment and is configured with an IP address to facilitate communication within that network.

Q.60How does a router determine the best path for data transmission?
Answer: A router uses routing tables to determine the best path for data transmission. These tables contain information about known networks and the associated next-hop routers, allowing the router to make informed forwarding decisions.

Q.61 What is the purpose of a VLAN (Virtual Local Area Network)?
Answer: VLANs are used to logically segment a network into smaller broadcast domains, improving network efficiency, security, and manageability. They group devices regardless of their physical location into broadcast domains.

Q.62 Explain the difference between a hub, a switch, and a router in a network.
Answer: A hub operates at the physical layer and broadcasts data to all connected devices. A switch operates at the data link layer, filtering and forwarding frames based on MAC addresses. A router operates at the network layer, making forwarding decisions based on IP addresses.

Q.63 What is STP (Spanning Tree Protocol) and why is it important in switched networks?
Answer: STP is a protocol that prevents loops in Ethernet networks by identifying redundant paths and blocking them. It ensures a loop-free topology, preventing broadcast storms and network instability.

Q.64 How does the MAC address table work in a switch?
Answer: The MAC address table in a switch maps MAC addresses to the corresponding switch ports. When a frame arrives, the switch uses this table to forward the frame only to the port where the destination MAC address is located, reducing unnecessary traffic.

Q.65 What is the purpose of the VTP (VLAN Trunking Protocol) in Cisco networking?
Answer: VTP is used to synchronize VLAN information across multiple switches in a network. It helps in maintaining consistent VLAN configurations, reducing the administrative overhead of manually configuring VLANs on each switch.

Q.66 Explain the concept of broadcast domains and collision domains in switched networks.
Answer: A broadcast domain is a logical division of a network where broadcast traffic is contained. A collision domain is the segment of a network where collisions can occur. Switches reduce collision domains, enhancing network efficiency.

Q.67 What is the difference between half-duplex and full-duplex communication in networking?

Answer: In half-duplex communication, devices can either send or receive data at a given time, but not simultaneously. In full-duplex communication, devices can send and receive data simultaneously, doubling the potential bandwidth.

Q.68 How does Port Security enhance network security in a switched environment?

Answer: Port Security restricts access to a switch port based on the MAC address of the connected device. It helps prevent unauthorized devices from connecting to the network and protects against MAC address spoofing.

Q.69 What is the purpose of the EtherChannel in Cisco networking?

Answer: EtherChannel is used to bundle multiple physical links into a single logical link, providing increased bandwidth and redundancy. It enhances fault tolerance and load balancing across the aggregated links.

Q.70 How does QoS (Quality of Service) play a role in switch configuration, and why is it important?

Answer: QoS prioritizes and manages network traffic to ensure that critical data gets higher priority. In a switch, QoS can be configured to prioritize certain types of traffic, such as voice or video, ensuring optimal performance for those applications.

Q.71 How do you create a VLAN on a Cisco switch?

Answer: To create a VLAN on a Cisco switch, use the **vlanvlan-id** command in global configuration mode. For example, **vlan 10** creates VLAN 10. After creating the VLAN, assign it to a switch interface using the **switchport access vlanvlan-id** command in interface configuration mode.

Q.72 What is the purpose of the "show vlan" command, and how can it be used in troubleshooting?

Answer: The "show vlan" command displays information about configured VLANs on a switch. It provides details such as VLAN names, VLAN IDs, and associated switch ports. In troubleshooting, this command helps verify VLAN configurations and quickly identify any misconfigurations.

Q.73 Explain the difference between access ports and trunk ports in VLAN configuration.

Answer: Access ports are used to connect end devices to a specific VLAN, while trunk ports carry traffic for multiple VLANs. Trunk ports use encapsulation protocols like 802.1Q to tag VLAN information on frames, allowing switches to differentiate between VLANs.

Q.74 What is the purpose of the "native VLAN" on a trunk port, and how is it configured?

Answer: The native VLAN on a trunk port is the VLAN that carries untagged traffic. It is essential for interoperability between switches. To configure the native VLAN, use the **switchport trunk native vlanvlan-id** command in interface configuration mode.

Q.75 How do you troubleshoot connectivity issues in a VLAN?

Answer: Troubleshooting VLAN connectivity involves checking VLAN configurations, verifying trunk links, ensuring correct VLAN assignments on switch ports, and using tools like the "show vlan" and "show interfaces" commands. Also, check for consistent VLAN configurations across interconnected switches.

Q.76 What is VLAN pruning, and why is it useful in a switched network?

Answer: VLAN pruning is a feature that prevents unnecessary traffic from being sent over trunk links. It dynamically removes VLANs from trunk links if they are not present on the destination switch, reducing unnecessary broadcast and multicast traffic.

Q.77 How can you prevent VLAN hopping attacks in a network?

Answer: VLAN hopping attacks involve an attacker gaining unauthorized access to a VLAN. To prevent such attacks, implement techniques like VLAN access control lists (VACLs), dynamic trunking protocol (DTP) security measures, and ensuring that unused ports are either disabled or placed in an unused VLAN.

Q.78 What is the purpose of the "VTP pruning" feature, and how does it work?

Answer: VTP pruning is used to optimize bandwidth usage by preventing unnecessary broadcast traffic from being forwarded over trunk links. It dynamically prunes VLANs that are not needed on a specific trunk, based on the VLAN information exchanged via VTP.

Q.79 Explain the concept of Voice VLAN and how it is configured.

Answer: Voice VLAN is used to separate voice and data traffic in a network. It allows a switch to assign a specific VLAN to voice traffic, ensuring quality of service for VoIP applications. To configure Voice VLAN, use the **switchport voice vlanvlan-id** command in interface configuration mode.

Q.80 How can you verify the operational status and statistics of a specific VLAN interface on a Cisco switch?

Answer: To verify the operational status and statistics of a specific VLAN interface, use the "show interfaces vlanvlan-id" command. This command provides information about the VLAN interface, including its status, input/output errors, and traffic statistics.

Q.81 What is the purpose of implementing password security on routers and switches?

Answer: Implementing password security on routers and switches helps control access to the devices, preventing unauthorized users from making configuration changes or accessing sensitive information. This includes setting strong enable passwords and configuring password encryption.

Q.82 Explain the significance of the "service password-encryption" command on a Cisco device.

Answer: The "service password-encryption" command is used to encrypt passwords stored in the device's configuration file. It enhances security by preventing plain-text password exposure, making it more challenging for unauthorized users to decipher passwords.

Q.83 How can you secure remote access to a router or switch using SSH (Secure Shell)?

Answer: To secure remote access using SSH, configure the device with an RSA key pair, enable SSH with the "ipssh version 2" command, and restrict access to specific IP addresses using access control lists (ACLs). This ensures encrypted and secure remote management.

Q.84 What is the purpose of the "login" and "login local" commands in line configuration mode?

Answer: The "login" command enables the login process on a specific line, while "login local" requires users to provide a locally configured username and password for access. This is commonly used for console or VTY lines to enhance authentication security.

Q.85 How can you protect against unauthorized configuration changes on a Cisco device?

Answer: Implement the "enable secret" command to set a strong encrypted password for privileged mode access. Additionally, configure access control lists (ACLs) to restrict access to the device's management interfaces and use the "login block-for" command to prevent brute-force attacks.

Q.86 Explain the concept of Port Security on a switch and how it enhances network security.

Answer: Port Security restricts access to a switch port based on the MAC address of connected devices. It helps prevent unauthorized devices from connecting to the network, reducing the risk of security breaches caused by rogue devices.

Q.87 What is the purpose of implementing DHCP Snooping on a switch, and how does it enhance security?

Answer: DHCP Snooping helps protect against rogue DHCP servers by filtering and validating DHCP messages on untrusted switch ports. It ensures that only authorized DHCP servers can assign IP addresses, preventing potential man-in-the-middle attacks.

Q.88 How can you mitigate the risk of VLAN hopping attacks on a switch?

Answer: Mitigate VLAN hopping attacks by disabling dynamic trunking protocol (DTP) on switch ports, manually configuring trunk ports, and using VLAN access control lists (VACLs) to control traffic between VLANs. Additionally, ensure that unused ports are either disabled or placed in an unused VLAN.

Q.89 Explain the role of Access Control Lists (ACLs) in router security.

Answer: ACLs in routers are used to control traffic based on source and destination IP addresses, protocols, and ports. They serve as a security mechanism by permitting or denying specific types of traffic, helping to protect the network from unauthorized access and potential threats.

Q.90 How can you protect against physical security threats to routers and switches?

Answer: Protect against physical threats by placing network devices in secure locations, using cable locks to prevent unauthorized removal, and implementing environmental controls to avoid overheating. Additionally, configure password protection on console ports to restrict physical access.

Q.91 What is an IPv4 address, and how is it structured?

Answer: An IPv4 address is a 32-bit numerical label assigned to each device participating in a computer network that uses the Internet Protocol for communication. It is divided into four octets, separated by dots, and represented in decimal format (e.g., 192.168.1.1).

Q.92 Differentiate between public and private IP addresses.

Answer: Public IP addresses are routable on the public internet, while private IP addresses are used within private networks and are not routable on the internet. Reserved ranges, such as 10.0.0.0/8, 172.16.0.0/12, and 192.168.0.0/16, are commonly used for private IP addresses.

Q.93 What is subnetting, and why is it used in IP networking?

Answer: Subnetting is the practice of dividing an IP network into smaller, more manageable sub-networks or subnets. It helps optimize network performance, improve security, and efficiently allocate IP addresses by grouping devices based on their logical or geographical proximity.

Q.94 Explain the purpose of the subnet mask in IPv4 addressing.

Answer: The subnet mask is used to divide an IP address into network and host portions. It helps routers determine the network to which an IP address belongs by masking the host part. For example, in the address 192.168.1.1 with a subnet mask of 255.255.255.0, the network is 192.168.1.0.

Q.95 What is CIDR (Classless Inter-Domain Routing), and how does it affect IP addressing?

Answer: CIDR is a method of IP address allocation and route aggregation that allows for more flexible use of IP addresses. It replaces traditional classful addressing with variable-length subnet masks, enabling more efficient use of IP addresses and reducing routing table size.

Q.96 Describe the purpose of the default gateway in an IP network.

Answer: The default gateway is the IP address of the router that connects a local network to other networks, including the internet. It serves as the exit point for traffic that needs to reach destinations outside the local network.

Q.97 How are IPv4 addresses classified into different classes, and what are the characteristics of each class?

Answer: IPv4 addresses are classified into five classes (A, B, C, D, and E) based on the range of the first octet. Each class has a different range of possible values and is intended for specific purposes. For example, Class A addresses are typically used for large networks, while Class C addresses are for smaller networks.

Q.98 What is the purpose of ARP (Address Resolution Protocol) in IPv4 networking?

Answer: ARP is used to map a known IP address to its corresponding MAC address on a local network. When a device wants to communicate with another device on the same subnet, it uses ARP to discover the MAC address associated with the target IP address.

Q.99 Explain the concept of DHCP (Dynamic Host Configuration Protocol) in IPv4 networks.

Answer: DHCP is a protocol used to automatically assign IP addresses and other network configuration parameters to devices on a network. It eliminates the need for manual IP address configuration, making network management more efficient.

Q.100 How do you troubleshoot IP address conflicts in a network?

Answer: IP address conflicts occur when two devices in the same network have the same IP address. To troubleshoot, use tools like the "arp" command to check for duplicate IP addresses, verify DHCP configurations, and ensure that static IP addresses are not assigned within the DHCP range.

Chapter 3: Interview Questions & Answers Part 3

Q.101 What is subnetting, and why is it essential in IP networking?

Answer: Subnetting is the process of dividing an IP network into smaller sub-networks to optimize address space, improve network efficiency, and enhance security by logically grouping devices.

Q.102 How do you calculate the number of subnets and hosts per subnet in a given IP address space?

Answer: Use the formula 2^n, where "n" is the number of subnet bits, to calculate the number of subnets. To calculate the number of hosts per subnet, use the formula 2^(32-n) - 2, subtracting 2 for the network and broadcast addresses.

Q.103 Explain the significance of the subnet mask in the subnetting process.

Answer: The subnet mask defines the boundary between the network and host portions of an IP address. It is crucial in subnetting to determine the size of each subnet and the number of hosts it can accommodate.

Q.104 How do you represent subnet masks in CIDR notation?

Answer: CIDR notation expresses subnet masks using a slash followed by the subnet prefix length. For example, a subnet mask of 255.255.255.0 is represented as "/24."

Q.105 What is the purpose of the network address and broadcast address in a subnet?

Answer: The network address represents the beginning of a subnet, and the broadcast address is the end. The network address is used to identify the subnet itself, while the broadcast address is used for sending messages to all hosts within that subnet.

Q.106 How can Variable Length Subnet Masking (VLSM) enhance the efficiency of IP address allocation?

Answer: VLSM allows for the use of different subnet mask lengths within the same network, enabling more efficient allocation of IP addresses by tailoring subnet sizes to the specific needs of different subnets.

Q.107 What is the difference between a fixed-length subnet mask and a variable-length subnet mask?

Answer: A fixed-length subnet mask uses the same subnet mask throughout the network, while a variable-length subnet mask allows for different subnet mask lengths, providing flexibility in subnet size.

Q.108 Explain the process of subnetting a Class C network address.

Answer: Subnetting a Class C network involves borrowing bits from the host portion of the address. The number of borrowed bits determines the number of subnets and hosts per subnet. Adjust the subnet mask accordingly.

Q.109 How do you identify the subnet to which an IP address belongs?

Answer: Use the logical AND operation between the IP address and subnet mask. The result is the network address. If the obtained network address matches the subnet, the IP address belongs to that subnet.

Q.110 What is Variable Length Subnet Masking (VLSM), and why is it important in networking?

Answer: VLSM is a subnetting technique that allows the use of different subnet mask lengths within the same network. It is crucial for optimizing IP address allocation by tailoring subnet sizes to match the specific requirements of different subnets.

Q.111 How does VLSM differ from traditional subnetting?

Answer: In traditional subnetting, a fixed-length subnet mask is used throughout the network. VLSM allows for flexibility by using subnet masks of varying lengths within the same network.

Q.112 Explain the process of implementing VLSM on a network.

Answer: To implement VLSM, identify the network's overall addressing needs, allocate IP addresses based on these needs, and assign subnet masks of different lengths to match the requirements of each subnet.

Q.113 What benefits does VLSM offer in terms of IP address conservation?

Answer: VLSM conserves IP addresses by allowing the allocation of smaller subnets where needed and larger subnets where more addresses are required. This results in more efficient use of address space.

Q.114 How can you determine the number of subnets and hosts per subnet using VLSM?

Answer: Calculate the number of subnets using the formula 2^n, where "n" is the number of subnet bits. For hosts per subnet, use the formula 2^(32-n) - 2, subtracting 2 for the network and broadcast addresses.

Q.115 Why is VLSM particularly useful in large networks with diverse requirements?

Answer: VLSM is beneficial in large networks because it allows network administrators to allocate IP addresses based on specific subnet requirements, ensuring optimal utilization of address space and efficient routing.

Q.116 How do routers handle VLSM in terms of routing tables?

Answer: Routers handle VLSM by recognizing different subnet masks within the same network. This enables routers to make more specific routing decisions based on subnet boundaries, reducing the size of routing tables.

Q.117 What challenges might arise when implementing VLSM in a network?

Answer: Challenges in VLSM implementation include careful planning to avoid wasting IP addresses, potential complexity in managing different subnet masks, and the need for accurate documentation to maintain the network efficiently.

Q.118 Can VLSM be applied to both IPv4 and IPv6 networks?

Answer: Yes, VLSM is applicable to both IPv4 and IPv6 networks. However, the notation and procedures differ between the two protocols.

Q.119 What is the primary motivation for transitioning from IPv4 to IPv6?

Answer: The primary motivation for transitioning to IPv6 is the exhaustion of IPv4 addresses. IPv6 provides a larger address space, accommodating the growing number of devices connected to the internet.

Q.120 Explain the structure of an IPv6 address.

Answer: An IPv6 address is a 128-bit hexadecimal address divided into eight groups of four hexadecimal digits separated by colons. For example, 2001:0db8:85a3:0000:0000:8a2e:0370:7334.

Q.121 How does IPv6 simplify address configuration compared to IPv4?

Answer: IPv6 simplifies address configuration through stateless address autoconfiguration (SLAAC), eliminating the need for DHCP in many cases. Hosts can generate their own addresses using the prefix advertised by routers.

Q.122 What is the purpose of the double-colon (::) notation in IPv6 addresses?

Answer: The double-colon notation is used to represent consecutive groups of zeros in an IPv6 address. It can only be used once in an address, simplifying the representation of long sequences of zeros.

Q.123 Describe the IPv6 unique local address space.

Answer: Unique local addresses (ULA) in IPv6 are similar to IPv4 private addresses. They are used for local communication within a site and are not routable on the global internet. The ULA prefix starts with "fc00::/7."

Q.124 How is subnetting handled in IPv6 compared to IPv4?

Answer: Subnetting in IPv6 is typically handled through the allocation of smaller portions of the assigned global prefix. Unlike IPv4, where subnet masks are variable, IPv6 uses a fixed 64-bit prefix for subnets.

Q.125 Explain the purpose of link-local addresses in IPv6.

Answer: Link-local addresses in IPv6 are used for communication on a single network segment or link. They are automatically configured on interfaces and have a prefix of "fe80::/10."

Q.126 What is the role of the anycast address in IPv6?

Answer: Anycast addresses in IPv6 are used to send a packet to the nearest of a group of servers providing the same service. The same anycast address is assigned to multiple devices, and the routing infrastructure determines the nearest one.

Q.127 How does Neighbor Discovery Protocol (NDP) replace functions performed by Address Resolution Protocol (ARP) in IPv4?

Answer: Neighbor Discovery Protocol (NDP) in IPv6 combines the functionalities of ARP, ICMP Router Discovery, and ICMP Redirect from IPv4. It performs address resolution, router discovery, and neighbor unreachability detection.

Q.128 Describe the process of manually configuring an IPv6 address on a device.

Answer: To manually configure an IPv6 address, use the "ipv6 address" command in interface configuration mode on a Cisco device. For example, "ipv6 address 2001:db8::1/64."

Q.129 How are DNS records structured for IPv6 addresses?

Answer: IPv6 addresses in DNS records are represented as hexadecimal strings enclosed in square brackets. For example, "[2001:0db8::1]."

Q.130 What is the purpose of the "ipv6 unicast-routing" command on Cisco routers?

Answer: The "ipv6 unicast-routing" command enables IPv6 routing on a Cisco router. Without this command, the router will not process IPv6 packets or forward them between interfaces.

Q.131 Explain the significance of the Unique Local Unicast IPv6 prefix (fd00::/8).

Answer: The Unique Local Unicast prefix (fd00::/8) is reserved for local communication within an organization. It is similar to IPv4 private addresses but designed for IPv6, providing address space that is not globally routable.

Q.132 How does Stateless DHCPv6 differ from Stateful DHCPv6?

Answer: Stateless DHCPv6 provides additional configuration information (like DNS server addresses) without assigning specific IPv6 addresses. Stateful DHCPv6 assigns IPv6 addresses along with other configuration parameters.

Q.133 How does IPv6 support better security compared to IPv4?

Answer: IPv6 supports better security through features like IPsec, which is mandatory in IPv6. IPsec provides authentication and encryption at the network layer, enhancing the overall security of communications.

Q.134 What is the primary function of a router in a network?

Answer: A router is a networking device that forwards data packets between different networks. It operates at the network layer (Layer 3) of the OSI model.

Q.135 Differentiate between static routing and dynamic routing.

Answer: Static routing involves manually configuring routes, while dynamic routing relies on routing protocols to automatically update and maintain routing tables.

Q.136 What is a routing table, and how does it influence the routing process?
Answer: A routing table is a database that contains information about the network topology. It is used by routers to determine the best path for forwarding packets to their destinations.

Q.137 Explain the difference between a routing protocol and a routed protocol.
Answer: A routing protocol is used by routers to exchange routing information, while a routed protocol is used to transmit data across the network. Examples of routing protocols include OSPF and EIGRP, while IPv4 and IPv6 are examples of routed protocols.

Q.138 What is a default route, and why is it useful in routing configurations?
Answer: A default route is a route used by a router when there is no specific route in the routing table for a destination. It is often used as a gateway of last resort, directing traffic to an exit point.

Q.139 How does a router differentiate between different types of routes in its routing table?
Answer: Routers use the concept of administrative distance to prioritize routes. Lower administrative distances indicate higher priority. For example, a directly connected route has a lower administrative distance than a static route.

Q.140 What is the purpose of the Routing Information Protocol (RIP), and how does it work?
Answer: RIP is a distance-vector routing protocol used to exchange routing information between routers. It calculates the best path to a destination based on the number of hops.

Q.141 How does a router handle a packet with an unknown destination IP address?
Answer: A router will drop the packet and generate an Internet Control Message Protocol (ICMP) "Destination Unreachable" message, indicating that the destination is unreachable.

Q.142 What is the purpose of the subnet mask in the routing process?
Answer: The subnet mask is used to determine the network and host portions of an IP address. It helps routers decide whether a destination IP address is on the same local network or a remote network.

Q.143 Explain the concept of a routing metric.
Answer: A routing metric is a value assigned to a route that reflects the cost or preference of that route. Different routing protocols use various metrics, such as hop count, bandwidth, or delay.

Q.144 How does a router handle a packet with a destination IP address within the same local network?

Answer: If the destination IP address is within the same local network, the router will use ARP (Address Resolution Protocol) to discover the MAC address of the destination device and forward the packet within the local network.

Q.145 What is the purpose of the "ip route" command in a router's configuration?

Answer: The "ip route" command is used to manually configure static routes on a router. It specifies the destination network and the next-hop address or exit interface.

Q.146 How does a router determine the best path among multiple routes to the same destination?

Answer: Routers use various factors, including the administrative distance, routing metric, and path cost, to determine the best path. The route with the lowest combined metric is selected.

Q.147 What is the significance of the loopback interface on a router?

Answer: The loopback interface (usually labeled as lo or lo0) is a virtual interface used to test the router's functionality. It is assigned a logical IP address and is always up, providing a stable reference point.

Q.148 How does the Border Gateway Protocol (BGP) differ from Interior Gateway Protocols (IGPs)?

Answer: BGP is an Exterior Gateway Protocol (EGP) used between different autonomous systems, while IGPs like OSPF and EIGRP are used within a single autonomous system.

Q.149 What is the purpose of the Autonomous System (AS) number in BGP?

Answer: The Autonomous System number uniquely identifies a collection of IP networks and routers under the control of a single entity. It is used in BGP to distinguish between different routing domains.

Q.150 Explain the concept of dynamic routing protocol convergence.

Answer: Dynamic routing protocol convergence refers to the process by which routers update their routing tables after a change in the network topology. It involves routers exchanging routing information until a consistent state is reached.

Chapter 4: Interview Questions & Answers Part 4

Q.151 How does a router handle a packet with a destination IP address outside its routing table?
Answer: If a router does not have a specific route for the destination IP address, it forwards the packet based on the default route, if available. Otherwise, it drops the packet and sends an ICMP "Destination Unreachable" message.

Q.152 What is the purpose of the "show ip route" command on a Cisco router?
Answer: The "show ip route" command displays the router's routing table, showing the routes learned via dynamic protocols, static routes, and connected networks, along with their metrics and next-hop information.

Q.153 How does a router determine the best path when using the Open Shortest Path First (OSPF) routing protocol?
Answer: OSPF uses the Shortest Path First (SPF) algorithm to determine the best path. The algorithm calculates the shortest path to each destination based on link costs and constructs a routing table.

Q.154 What is Routing Information Protocol (RIP), and which version is commonly used in IP networks?
Answer: RIP is a distance-vector routing protocol used to exchange routing information between routers. RIP version 2 (RIPv2) is commonly used in IP networks.

Q.155 Describe the key characteristics of RIP as a routing protocol.
Answer: RIP is a classful routing protocol with a maximum hop count of 15. It uses the Bellman-Ford algorithm to determine the best path to a destination based on hop count.

Q.156 What is the purpose of RIP's split horizon mechanism?
Answer: Split horizon is a mechanism in RIP that prevents a router from advertising routes back out on the interface from which they were learned. It helps avoid routing loops.

Q.157 Explain the concept of route poisoning in RIP.
Answer: Route poisoning is a technique in RIP where a router advertises a route with an infinite metric (16) to indicate that the route is unreachable. It aids in quickly propagating information about network changes.

Q.158 How does RIP prevent routing loops using the holddown timer?
Answer: The holddown timer is a feature in RIP that prevents the router from accepting route updates for a specified period after detecting a route change. This helps stabilize the network and avoid temporary routing loops.

Q.159 What is the purpose of the RIP authentication feature, and how is it configured?

Answer: RIP authentication ensures that only authorized routers can participate in RIP updates. It is configured by setting a simple text password using the "ip rip authentication key-chain" command.

Q.160 Explain the difference between RIP version 1 (RIPv1) and RIP version 2 (RIPv2).

Answer: RIPv2 includes improvements over RIPv1, such as support for variable-length subnet masks (VLSM), route summarization, and authentication. RIPv2 is more versatile and suitable for modern networks.

Q.161 What is the maximum hop count allowed in RIP, and why is this limit significant?

Answer: RIP has a maximum hop count of 15. This limit is significant because any route with a hop count greater than 15 is considered unreachable, preventing the formation of routing loops.

Q.162 How does RIP handle route updates and what information is included in an RIP update?

Answer: RIP sends periodic updates (every 30 seconds by default) containing information about directly connected networks. Updates include the destination network, subnet mask, and hop count.

Q.163 What role does the "ip rip send version" command play in RIP configuration?

Answer: The "ip rip send version" command specifies the version of RIP used to send updates. It can be used to force the router to send updates in RIPv1 or RIPv2 format.

Q.164 How does RIP determine the best path to a destination network?

Answer: RIP determines the best path based on the hop count. The route with the fewest hops is considered the best path to the destination.

Q.165 Explain the purpose of the "ip rip triggered" command in RIP configuration.

Answer: The "ip rip triggered" command enables triggered updates in RIP. These updates are sent immediately in response to a topology change, reducing convergence time.

Q.166 What is the significance of the "ip rip authentication mode" command in RIP authentication?

Answer: The "ip rip authentication mode" command sets the authentication mode for RIP. It can be set to "text" for a simple plaintext password or "md5" for a more secure MD5 hash-based authentication.

Q.167 How does RIP handle networks with a subnet mask longer than the classful boundary (e.g., using VLSM)?

Answer: RIPv2 supports Variable Length Subnet Masks (VLSM) and can carry subnet mask information in its updates, allowing it to handle networks with a subnet mask longer than the classful boundary.

Q.168 What is the purpose of route summarization in RIP, and how is it configured?

Answer: Route summarization reduces the size of the routing table by aggregating multiple routes into a single summary route. In RIP, summarization is configured using the "ip summary-address" command.

Q.169 Explain the role of the "passive-interface" command in RIP configuration.
Answer: The "passive-interface" command in RIP prevents the router from sending updates on a specific interface. It is useful for interfaces that don't need to participate in routing updates, like loopback interfaces.

Q.170 How does RIP use the hold-down timer to avoid instability after a network change?
Answer: The hold-down timer is activated when a route is removed from the routing table. During this timer, the router ignores any new updates for the same route, preventing it from accepting potentially incorrect information.

Q.171 What is the purpose of the "clear ip rip" command, and when might it be used?
Answer: The "clear ip rip" command is used to reset RIP processes on a router. It can be used to force an immediate update of RIP information or to clear stale or outdated routing information.

Q.172 Explain the role of split horizon with poison reverse in RIP.
Answer: Split horizon with poison reverse is a mechanism in RIP where a router advertises a route back to the same router from which it was learned, but with an infinite metric. It helps prevent routing loops.

Q.173 How does RIP contribute to network convergence, and what factors affect the convergence time?
Answer: RIP contributes to network convergence by quickly propagating information about network changes. The factors affecting convergence time include the update timer, hold-down timer, and triggered updates in response to changes in the network topology.

Q.174 What is Enhanced Interior Gateway Routing Protocol (EIGRP), and how does it differ from traditional distance-vector protocols?
Answer: EIGRP is an advanced distance-vector routing protocol developed by Cisco. It differs from traditional distance-vector protocols by incorporating features such as fast convergence, support for variable-length subnet masks (VLSM), and reduced bandwidth consumption.

Q.175 How does EIGRP calculate the composite metric for route selection?
Answer: EIGRP uses a composite metric called the "EIGRP metric" or "composite cost," which considers factors like bandwidth, delay, reliability, load, and maximum transmission unit (MTU). The metric is calculated using the formula: metric = [K1 * bandwidth + (K2 * bandwidth) / (256 - load) + K3 * delay] * [K5 / (reliability + K4)].

Q.176 What are the main components of an EIGRP router ID, and how is it selected?

Answer: The EIGRP router ID is composed of the highest IP address of any of its active interfaces. If the router has no active interfaces, the router ID can be manually configured.

Q.177 Explain the purpose of the EIGRP neighbor table.
Answer: The EIGRP neighbor table, also known as the adjacency table, maintains information about neighboring routers, including their IP addresses, interface, hold time, and the state of the relationship (active, passive, or established).

Q.178 How does EIGRP use the Diffusing Update Algorithm (DUAL) to achieve loop-free routing?
Answer: DUAL is used by EIGRP to ensure loop-free routing. It constructs a topology table and calculates the best route based on a successor (best path) and feasible successors (backup paths) to prevent routing loops.

Q.179 What is the purpose of the EIGRP Reliable Transport Protocol (RTP)?
Answer: RTP is a protocol used by EIGRP to provide reliable, ordered delivery of EIGRP packets between routers. It ensures that updates are delivered in the correct order and acknowledged.

Q.180 Explain the role of the EIGRP hello packets in maintaining neighbor relationships.
Answer: EIGRP hello packets are used to discover and maintain neighbor relationships. Routers exchange hello packets to establish and verify neighbor relationships, and the information in these packets helps routers determine if neighbors are reachable.

Q.181 What is the EIGRP feasible distance, and how is it used in route selection?
Answer: The EIGRP feasible distance is the metric of the best path to reach a destination. It is used to determine the successor route, which is the best path to a destination based on the lowest feasible distance.

Q.182 How does EIGRP support route summarization, and why is it beneficial?
Answer: EIGRP supports route summarization by aggregating multiple contiguous networks into a single summary route. This reduces the size of the routing table and enhances network efficiency.

Q.183 What is OSPF, and what makes it a link-state routing protocol?
Answer: OSPF, or Open Shortest Path First, is a link-state routing protocol that uses a database of link-state information to build a topology map of the entire network. It calculates the shortest path to each destination based on this map.

Q.184 How does OSPF determine the cost of a link, and why is this cost significant?

Answer: OSPF uses the bandwidth of a link to determine its cost. The cost is inversely proportional to the bandwidth, meaning higher bandwidth results in a lower cost. The cost is significant because OSPF uses it to calculate the shortest path to a destination.

Q.185 What is the purpose of OSPF's Designated Router (DR) and Backup Designated Router (BDR) in multi-access networks?

Answer: In multi-access networks like Ethernet, OSPF elects a Designated Router (DR) and a Backup Designated Router (BDR) to reduce the number of adjacencies and control OSPF traffic. The DR and BDR roles help in efficient neighbor relationships.

Q.186 Explain the OSPF Hello protocol and its role in neighbor discovery.

Answer: OSPF uses Hello packets to discover and establish neighbor relationships. Hello packets contain information like router ID, area ID, and the list of neighbors. Routers must agree on certain parameters in Hello packets to become neighbors.

Q.187 How does OSPF prevent routing loops through the use of the Shortest Path First (SPF) algorithm?

Answer: OSPF uses the SPF algorithm to calculate the shortest path to each destination. The algorithm ensures that there are no loops in the resulting OSPF routing table.

Q.188 What is the OSPF router ID, and how is it selected?

Answer: The OSPF router ID uniquely identifies a router within an OSPF Autonomous System (AS). It is a 32-bit value, often derived from the highest IP address of any of the router's active interfaces. If not set manually, OSPF will select the highest IP address.

Q.189 Explain the concept of OSPF Areas and their significance in OSPF design.

Answer: OSPF uses Areas to logically partition large networks into smaller, manageable segments. Areas reduce the size of OSPF databases, limit the scope of route advertisements, and improve overall scalability and network efficiency.

Q.190 How does OSPF handle route summarization, and why is it essential in OSPF deployment?

Answer: OSPF allows for route summarization at area boundaries. Summarization reduces the size of OSPF databases and routing tables, leading to more efficient network operation.

Q.191 What is the OSPF Link-State Database (LSDB), and how does it contribute to OSPF routing?

Answer: The OSPF Link-State Database (LSDB) is a database containing information about all routers and links within an OSPF area. It is used by routers to build a topology map and calculate the shortest path to each destination.

Q.192 What is Border Gateway Protocol (BGP), and what is its primary role in the Internet?

Answer: BGP is a standardized exterior gateway protocol used to exchange routing information between different autonomous systems (ASes) on the Internet. Its primary role is to facilitate the exchange of routing and reachability information between these autonomous systems.

Q.193 Differentiate between Interior Gateway Protocols (IGPs) and Exterior Gateway Protocols (EGPs), and where does BGP fall in this classification?

Answer: IGPs, such as OSPF and EIGRP, are used within a single autonomous system, while EGPs, like BGP, are used to exchange routing information between different autonomous systems. BGP is categorized as an EGP.

Q.194 What is the Autonomous System (AS) in the context of BGP, and why is it important?

Answer: An Autonomous System (AS) is a collection of IP networks and routers under the control of a single organization, sharing a common routing policy. BGP uses AS numbers to uniquely identify these autonomous systems.

Q.195 Explain the key difference between eBGP (External BGP) and iBGP (Internal BGP).

Answer:eBGP is used to exchange routing information between different autonomous systems, while iBGP is used to exchange routing information within the same autonomous system. Both are forms of BGP but serve different purposes.

Q.196 How does BGP ensure loop prevention in the context of AS path attributes?

Answer: BGP uses the AS path attribute to prevent routing loops. When a BGP router advertises a route, it appends its own AS number to the AS path. If a router receives an update with its own AS number in the AS path, it will reject the route to prevent loops.

Q.197 What is the purpose of the BGP Next-Hop attribute, and how is it used in BGP routing?

Answer: The BGP Next-Hop attribute indicates the next-hop IP address to reach the destination specified in the BGP update. Unlike interior gateway protocols, BGP does not modify the next-hop IP address by default.

Q.198 How does BGP determine the best path to a destination network, and what are the criteria involved in the decision-making process?

Answer: BGP uses the path selection process based on attributes such as the next-hop, AS path, origin code, and MED (Multi-Exit Discriminator) values. The router selects the path with the lowest aggregated value for these attributes.

Q.199 Explain the significance of the BGP Local Preference attribute.

Answer: BGP Local Preference is used within an autonomous system to influence the outbound routing decision. It is a non-transitive attribute, and higher values indicate a more preferred route.

Q.200 What is the role of the BGP Weight attribute, and how is it used in route selection?

Answer: BGP Weight is a Cisco-specific attribute used to influence the outbound route selection. Higher Weight values are preferred. Unlike other BGP attributes, Weight is not propagated to other routers outside the local AS.

Chapter 5: Interview Questions & Answers Part 5

Q.201 How does BGP handle route aggregation, and what is the purpose of the "aggregate-address" command?

Answer: BGP handles route aggregation by summarizing routes into a single, more specific route. The "aggregate-address" command is used to configure route aggregation in BGP.

Q.202 Explain the BGP Multi-Exit Discriminator (MED) attribute and its role in path selection.

Answer: BGP MED is used to influence the inbound route selection process. It represents the desirability of a route from a neighboring AS. Lower MED values are preferred, and routers use MED to choose the best entry point into an AS.

Q.203 How does BGP support route reflection in large-scale networks, and what is the purpose of the "bgp cluster-id" command?

Answer: BGP route reflection is used in large-scale networks to reduce the number of required iBGPpeerings. The "bgp cluster-id" command is used to configure the BGP cluster ID, helping to identify route reflectors.

Q.204 What is the BGP Confederation feature, and how does it address the issue of scalability in large autonomous systems?

Answer: BGP Confederation is another method to address the scalability issue in large autonomous systems. It divides the AS into sub-ASes, treating them as internal entities. BGP Confederation helps in reducing the number of iBGPpeerings.

Q.205 How does BGP handle route filtering, and what is the purpose of the "neighbor distribute-list" command?

Answer: BGP can filter routes based on access lists using the "neighbor distribute-list" command. This allows administrators to control which routes are advertised or received by a BGP neighbor.

Q.206 What is the BGP Route Distinguisher (RD) and Route Target (RT), and how are they used in the context of MPLS VPNs?

Answer: BGP Route Distinguisher (RD) is a 64-bit value used to distinguish between different VPNs. BGP Route Target (RT) is used to associate routes with specific VPNs. Together, they enable BGP to carry VPN information in MPLS VPNs.

Q.207 What is the primary goal of network security?

Answer: The primary goal of network security is to protect the confidentiality, integrity, and availability of data within a network.

Q.208 Explain the concept of the CIA Triad in the context of network security.

Answer: The CIA Triad stands for Confidentiality, Integrity, and Availability. It is a fundamental framework in network security where confidentiality protects data from unauthorized access, integrity ensures data is accurate and unmodified, and availability ensures data is accessible when needed.

Q.209 What is the role of firewalls in network security?

Answer: Firewalls act as a barrier between a trusted internal network and untrusted external networks, controlling and monitoring incoming and outgoing network traffic based on predetermined security rules.

Q.210 How does encryption contribute to network security, and what are common encryption algorithms used?

Answer: Encryption secures data by converting it into a format that can only be deciphered with the appropriate key. Common encryption algorithms include AES (Advanced Encryption Standard), DES (Data Encryption Standard), and RSA (Rivest–Shamir–Adleman).

Q.211 Explain the purpose of intrusion detection systems (IDS) and intrusion prevention systems (IPS).

Answer: Intrusion Detection Systems (IDS) monitor network traffic for suspicious activities or security policy violations, while Intrusion Prevention Systems (IPS) not only detect but also take proactive measures to prevent or block such activities.

Q.212 What is a Virtual Private Network (VPN), and how does it enhance network security?

Answer: A VPN creates a secure, encrypted connection over an unsecured network, such as the internet. It enhances network security by ensuring data confidentiality during transmission over potentially insecure networks.

Q.213 Describe the role of access control in network security.

Answer: Access control regulates and restricts user access to network resources based on their identity and permissions. It prevents unauthorized users from accessing sensitive information.

Q.214 What are the differences between symmetric and asymmetric encryption?

Answer: In symmetric encryption, the same key is used for both encryption and decryption, while in asymmetric encryption, different keys are used for these processes (public key for encryption, private key for decryption).

Q.215 What is the purpose of Network Address Translation (NAT) in network security?

Answer: NAT is used to hide internal network IP addresses by translating them to a single public IP address when communicating with external networks. This helps enhance security by obfuscating internal network details.

Q.216 What is the primary purpose of an Access Control List (ACL) in networking?

Answer: An Access Control List (ACL) is used to control and filter network traffic by permitting or denying packets based on specified criteria, such as source and destination IP addresses, protocols, and ports.

Q.217 Differentiate between Standard ACLs and Extended ACLs.

Answer: Standard ACLs filter traffic based only on source IP addresses, while Extended ACLs allow filtering based on source and destination IP addresses, protocols, and ports.

Q.219 How are ACLs processed, and why is the order of ACL entries crucial?

Answer: ACLs are processed in order, top-down. Once a match is found, the device applies the corresponding action, and further processing stops. The order is crucial as the first match determines the fate of the packet.

Q.220 What is the significance of the implicit "deny any" statement in ACLs?

Answer: Every ACL, whether Standard or Extended, has an implicit "deny any" statement at the end. If a packet doesn't match any preceding rules, it is denied by default.

Q.221 Explain the syntax for configuring a Standard ACL.

Answer: The syntax is: **access-list {1-99} {permit|deny} {source}**. The range for Standard ACLs is 1 to 99.

Q.222 How does an Extended ACL differ from a Standard ACL in terms of syntax?

Answer: The syntax for Extended ACLs includes additional parameters for specifying source and destination IP addresses, protocols, and ports. Example: **access-list {100-199} {permit|deny} {protocol} {source} {destination} {eq|gt|lt} {port}**.

Q.223 What is the purpose of the wildcard mask in ACLs, and how is it used?

Answer: The wildcard mask is used in ACLs to indicate which bits of the address should be checked. In binary, 0 means the bit must match, and 1 means the bit is ignored.

Q.224 How can you apply an ACL to an interface on a router?

Answer: Use the **ip access-group** command followed by the ACL number and direction (in or out) on the interface. For example: **ip access-group 1 in**.

Q.225 Explain the concept of Named ACLs and their advantages over numbered ACLs.

Answer: Named ACLs use alphanumeric identifiers instead of numbers, offering better readability and flexibility. They can be edited without changing the order, and multiple ACLs can coexist on a device.

Q.226 What is a VPN, and why would an organization implement it?

Answer: A VPN, or Virtual Private Network, is a secure and encrypted connection established over a public network, typically the internet. Organizations implement VPNs to ensure secure communication, allowing remote users or branch offices to connect to the corporate network securely.

Q.227 Differentiate between Remote Access VPNs and Site-to-Site VPNs.

Answer: Remote Access VPNs are designed for individual users connecting to a network remotely, while Site-to-Site VPNs connect entire networks, enabling secure communication between different locations.

Q.228 How does IPSec contribute to the security of a VPN, and what are its key components?

Answer: IPSec (Internet Protocol Security) is a protocol suite used to secure communication at the network layer. Its key components are the Authentication Header (AH) and the Encapsulating Security Payload (ESP), providing authentication, integrity, and encryption.

Q.229 Explain the concept of Split Tunneling in VPNs.

Answer: Split Tunneling is a VPN configuration that allows users to access both the corporate network and the internet directly. While it can improve performance, it introduces potential security risks.

Q.230 What is the role of a VPN concentrator in a VPN architecture?

Answer: A VPN concentrator aggregates multiple VPN connections and manages their traffic. It serves as a central point for processing VPN connections, providing scalability and efficient management.

Q.231 How can Quality of Service (QoS) be implemented in VPNs, and why is it important?

Answer: QoS in VPNs involves prioritizing certain types of traffic to ensure optimal performance. It is important for maintaining the quality of real-time applications like voice and video over VPN connections.

Q.232What considerations should be taken into account when choosing between SSL/TLS and IPSec VPNs for remote access scenarios?

Answer: Consider factors such as ease of use, compatibility with devices, and security requirements. SSL/TLS VPNs are often preferred for user-friendly remote access, while IPSec VPNs offer a broader range of security features.

Q.233 Explain the role of Network Address Translation (NAT) in VPNs and potential challenges it may introduce.

Answer: NAT is often used in VPNs to translate private IP addresses to public IP addresses. Challenges may arise in scenarios where NAT alters source or destination addresses, impacting VPN traffic.

Q.234 How can a VPN enhance security when using public Wi-Fi networks?

Answer: VPNs encrypt traffic, providing a secure tunnel even on untrusted networks like public Wi-Fi. This prevents unauthorized access to data transmitted between the user and the VPN server.

Q.235What is Network Address Translation (NAT)?

Answer: NAT is a technique that allows multiple devices in a private network to share a single public IP address for accessing resources on the internet.

Q.236 Explain the difference between Static NAT and Dynamic NAT.

Answer: Static NAT maps a private IP address to a specific public IP address, while Dynamic NAT assigns an available public IP address from a pool to a private IP address dynamically.

Q.237 What is the purpose of NAT in an enterprise network?

Answer: NAT is used to conserve public IP addresses, enhance network security, and facilitate communication between devices on a private network and the internet.

Q.238 Describe the types of NAT translations.

Answer: Types of NAT translations include Static NAT, Dynamic NAT, Overloading (PAT), and Inside Local, Inside Global, Outside Local, Outside Global translations.

Q.239 What is Overloading in NAT?

Answer: Overloading, also known as Port Address Translation (PAT), allows multiple private IP addresses to be mapped to a single public IP address using different ports.

Q.240 How does Dynamic PAT (Overloading) work?

Answer: Dynamic PAT maps multiple private IP addresses to a single public IP address by using different source ports for each connection.

Q.241 What is the difference between Inside Local and Inside Global addresses in NAT?

Answer: Inside Local refers to the private IP address of a device within the local network, while Inside Global is the translated public IP address seen by devices outside the local network.

Q.242 Explain the term "NAT table" or "translation table."

Answer: The NAT table keeps track of the mapping between private and public IP addresses, including information such as port numbers and the type of translation being used.

Q.243 How does NAT enhance security in a network?

Answer: NAT hides the internal network structure by using a single public IP address for outbound traffic, making it more challenging for external entities to directly access devices within the private network.

Q.244 What is Dynamic NAT Exemption?

Answer: Dynamic NAT Exemption (also known as NAT 0 or NAT Exempt) is a configuration that exempts certain traffic from NAT translation. This is often used for traffic between specific internal networks.

Q.245 Can NAT be bidirectional?

Answer: Yes, NAT is bidirectional, meaning it can translate both source and destination IP addresses and ports.

Q.246 How does NAT affect end-to-end connectivity?

Answer: NAT can impact end-to-end connectivity by introducing a middle device that modifies IP addresses, potentially causing issues with certain applications that rely on direct IP communication.

Q.247 What is the purpose of the "ipnat inside" and "ipnat outside" commands?

Answer: These commands are used to designate interfaces as either inside or outside interfaces, helping the router determine which addresses to translate.

Q.248Explain the term "NAT overload."

Answer: NAT overload, or Port Address Translation (PAT), allows multiple private IP addresses to be mapped to a single public IP address using different source ports.

Q.249 How does NAT handle incoming traffic initiated from the internet?

Answer: For incoming traffic, NAT uses the NAT table to determine the correct private IP address and port to which to forward the incoming packets.

Q.250 What is the role of Network Address and Port Translation (NAPT)?

Answer: NAPT is a type of NAT that maps multiple private IP addresses to a single public IP address using unique source ports, allowing for more efficient use of public IP addresses.

Chapter 6: Interview Questions & Answers Part 6

Q.251 What are the benefits and challenges of using NAT?

Answer: Benefits include conservation of public IP addresses and enhanced security. Challenges may include issues with certain applications, especially those requiring direct communication.

Q.252 How does NAT impact traceability in network troubleshooting?

Answer: NAT can complicate traceability, as it masks the original source IP addresses in outgoing packets. Proper logging and documentation are essential for effective troubleshooting.

Q.253 When might you use Static NAT instead of Dynamic NAT?

Answer: Static NAT is often used when you have a specific device that requires a consistent mapping to a public IP address, such as a web server or an email server.

Q.254 What considerations are important when designing a NAT implementation for scalability?

Answer: Scalable NAT designs should consider the size of the address pool, the number of devices, potential future growth, and the type of NAT (Static, Dynamic, PAT) based on network requirements.

Q.255 What is a firewall, and what is its primary purpose in a network?

Answer: A firewall is a network security device that monitors and controls incoming and outgoing network traffic based on predetermined security rules. Its primary purpose is to establish a barrier between a trusted internal network and untrusted external networks.

Q.256 Differentiate between stateful and stateless firewalls.

Answer: A stateful firewall keeps track of the state of active connections and makes decisions based on the context of the traffic. A stateless firewall filters packets based solely on source and destination information, without considering the state of the connection.

Q.257 What is Access Control List (ACL) in the context of firewall configuration?

Answer: An Access Control List (ACL) is a set of rules or filters used by a firewall to permit or deny traffic based on specified criteria such as source and destination IP addresses, ports, and protocols.

Q.258 Explain the difference between an incoming rule and an outgoing rule in a firewall configuration.

Answer: An incoming rule controls traffic entering the network, while an outgoing rule regulates traffic leaving the network. Both are essential for securing network communications.

Q.259 How does Network Address Translation (NAT) play a role in firewall configuration?

Answer: NAT is often used in firewall configurations to map private IP addresses to a single public IP address, providing additional security by hiding internal network details from external entities.

Q.260 What is the purpose of a DMZ (Demilitarized Zone) in firewall design?
Answer: A DMZ is an isolated network segment placed between the internal network and an external network, typically hosting servers accessible from the internet. It provides an additional layer of security.

Q.261 How can a firewall prevent common attacks such as DDoS and port scanning?
Answer: Firewalls can implement rate limiting for connection requests, blocking IP addresses after a certain threshold is reached, and by configuring rules to deny traffic associated with known attack patterns.

Q.262 Explain the concept of a proxy firewall.
Answer: A proxy firewall acts as an intermediary between internal clients and external servers. It intercepts requests from internal clients, makes the requests on their behalf, and forwards the responses, providing an additional layer of security.

Q.263 What is the role of stateful inspection in firewall security?
Answer: Stateful inspection monitors the state of active connections and makes decisions based on the context of the traffic, ensuring that only legitimate and established connections are permitted.

Q.264 How can a firewall be configured to allow remote access to internal resources?
Answer: By configuring Virtual Private Network (VPN) or Remote Desktop Protocol (RDP) rules, a firewall can allow secure remote access to internal resources.

Q.265 Describe the process of setting up a basic firewall rule to allow specific incoming traffic.
Answer: To set up a basic firewall rule, you define the source and destination addresses, specify the allowed ports and protocols, and decide whether to allow or deny the traffic.

Q.266 What is the difference between a stateful firewall and an application layer firewall?
Answer: A stateful firewall operates at the network layer and considers the state of active connections. An application layer firewall, also known as a proxy firewall, operates at the application layer and can inspect and filter traffic based on specific applications.

Q.267 How does a firewall handle traffic that does not match any rule?
Answer: By default, a firewall will deny traffic that does not match any rule. It is essential to have a default deny rule to ensure that only explicitly allowed traffic is permitted.

Q.268 What is the role of Intrusion Prevention System (IPS) in conjunction with a firewall?

Answer: An Intrusion Prevention System (IPS) works alongside a firewall to actively monitor and analyze network traffic for potential threats, preventing malicious activity in real-time.

Q.269 How can a firewall be configured to log and monitor network activity?

Answer: By enabling logging features, a firewall can record information about allowed and denied traffic, providing administrators with valuable insights into network activity for monitoring and analysis.

Q.270 What is the difference between stateful firewall and stateless firewall in terms of packet inspection?

Answer: A stateful firewall examines the context and state of network connections, allowing or denying traffic based on the connection's state. A stateless firewall filters packets based on predefined rules without considering the state of the connection.

Q.271 How can a firewall mitigate the risk of unauthorized access to sensitive data?

Answer: By implementing strong access control rules, encrypting communication channels, and regularly updating firewall policies, a firewall can significantly reduce the risk of unauthorized access to sensitive data.

Q.272 What are the potential drawbacks of using a firewall?

Answer: Drawbacks may include performance impact, potential for misconfigurations leading to security gaps, and the need for ongoing monitoring and updates to ensure effectiveness against evolving threats.

Q.273 How can a firewall protect against malware and malicious content?

Answer: By incorporating content filtering and antivirus features, a firewall can inspect web and email traffic for malware, preventing the download or execution of malicious content.

Q.274 What is the importance of regular firewall rule reviews and updates?

Answer: Regular reviews and updates of firewall rules are crucial to adapting to changing network requirements, closing security gaps, and ensuring the firewall remains an effective barrier against emerging threats.

Q.275 What is a Wireless LAN (WLAN)?

Answer: A Wireless LAN (WLAN) is a type of local area network that uses radio waves rather than physical cables to connect devices, allowing for wireless communication.

Q.276 Explain the basic components of a WLAN.

Answer: The basic components of a WLAN include wireless access points (APs), wireless clients (devices), and the wireless infrastructure that facilitates communication between them.

Q.277 What is SSID, and why is it essential in WLANs?

Answer: SSID (Service Set Identifier) is a unique identifier that distinguishes one WLAN from another. It is crucial for devices to connect to the correct network and is a key element in WLAN security.

Q.278 Differentiate between infrastructure mode and ad-hoc mode in WLANs.

Answer: Infrastructure mode involves connecting wireless clients through a central wireless access point (AP), while ad-hoc mode allows devices to connect directly to each other without the need for an AP.

Q.279 What is the purpose of a Basic Service Set (BSS) in WLANs?

Answer: A Basic Service Set (BSS) is the basic building block of a WLAN and consists of a wireless client and an access point (AP) in infrastructure mode.

Q.280 How does a WLAN handle data collisions?

Answer: WLANs use protocols like CSMA/CA (Carrier Sense Multiple Access with Collision Avoidance) to avoid data collisions. Devices listen before transmitting to determine if the channel is clear.

Q.281 Explain the role of a Wireless Distribution System (WDS) in WLANs.

Answer: WDS is used to interconnect access points wirelessly, forming a bridge between different parts of the WLAN and extending its coverage.

Q.282 What is the significance of wireless channels in WLANs?

Answer: Wireless channels are specific frequencies within the radio spectrum used by WLANs. Proper channel selection helps minimize interference and optimize performance.

Q.283 What is the purpose of a beacon frame in WLAN communication?

Answer: Beacon frames are periodically transmitted by access points to announce their presence and provide information about the network, including the SSID and supported data rates.

Q.284 How does Wi-Fi security work in WLANs?

Answer: Wi-Fi security involves encryption protocols like WPA2 (Wi-Fi Protected Access 2) or WPA3 to secure data during transmission. Additionally, measures like MAC filtering and disabling SSID broadcast enhance security.

Q.285 What is the role of a wireless controller in WLAN management?

Answer: A wireless controller is a centralized device that manages multiple access points in a WLAN. It helps with configuration, monitoring, and security enforcement.

Q.286 How does beamforming improve WLAN performance?

Answer: Beamforming is a technique that focuses wireless signals toward specific devices, enhancing signal strength and coverage, leading to improved performance in WLANs.

Q.287 What is the purpose of Quality of Service (QoS) in WLANs?

Answer: QoS in WLANs prioritizes certain types of traffic to ensure that critical applications, such as voice or video, receive preferential treatment for better performance.

Q.288 Explain the concept of handover or roaming in WLANs.

Answer: Roaming allows a wireless client to maintain a continuous connection while moving between different access points within the same WLAN.

Q.289 How does WPA3 improve WLAN security over previous versions?

Answer: WPA3 introduces stronger encryption algorithms and enhances security features to protect against emerging threats, providing a more robust security framework for WLANs.

Q.290 What is the role of a wireless site survey in WLAN deployment?

Answer: A wireless site survey involves analyzing the physical environment to determine optimal access point placement, minimizing interference, and ensuring comprehensive WLAN coverage.

Q.291 What are the common challenges in WLAN deployment, and how can they be mitigated?

Answer: Challenges include interference, signal attenuation, and security concerns. These can be addressed through proper channel planning, strategic access point placement, and robust security measures.

Q.292 How does 802.11ax (Wi-Fi 6) improve WLAN performance?

Answer: 802.11ax introduces technologies like OFDMA (Orthogonal Frequency Division Multiple Access) and MU-MIMO (Multi-User, Multiple Input, Multiple Output) to enhance efficiency, capacity, and overall performance in WLANs.

Q.293 What is the role of a captive portal in WLANs?

Answer: A captive portal is a web page that users must interact with before accessing the internet through a WLAN. It often involves authentication or acceptance of terms and conditions.

Q.294 How does a Mesh WLAN architecture function?

Answer: In a Mesh WLAN, each access point is interconnected, forming a self-healing and resilient network. If one access point fails, data can still be transmitted through alternative paths, improving reliability.

Q.295 What steps are involved in configuring a basic wireless network?

Answer: Configuring a basic wireless network involves setting up the wireless access point (AP), defining the SSID, configuring security settings, and connecting wireless clients.

Q.296 How can you enhance the security of a wireless network?
Answer: Security measures include enabling WPA3 encryption, using strong and unique passwords, implementing MAC filtering, disabling SSID broadcast, and regularly updating firmware.

Q.297 Explain the purpose of MAC filtering in wireless network security.
Answer: MAC filtering restricts access to a wireless network based on the MAC addresses of devices, allowing only specified devices to connect and enhancing overall security.

Q.298 What is the significance of disabling SSID broadcast in wireless network security?
Answer: Disabling SSID broadcast prevents the network's name from being publicly visible, adding an extra layer of security by making it less discoverable to potential attackers.

Q.299 How does WPA3 differ from WPA2 in terms of wireless security?
Answer: WPA3 introduces stronger encryption algorithms and security features, making it more resistant to attacks compared to WPA2.

Q.300 What is the purpose of setting up a Guest Network in a wireless environment?
Answer: A Guest Network provides a separate and isolated network for guests, ensuring they have internet access while protecting the main network from potential security risks.

Chapter 7: Interview Questions & Answers Part 7

Q.301 How can you prevent unauthorized access to a wireless network?
Answer: To prevent unauthorized access, use strong encryption (WPA3), employ strong passwords, enable MAC filtering, and regularly audit and update security settings.

Q.302 Explain the concept of a captive portal in wireless network security.
Answer: A captive portal is a login page that users must interact with before gaining access to the network. It often involves authentication or acceptance of terms and conditions.

Q.303 What is the role of the Wireless Intrusion Prevention System (WIPS) in securing wireless networks?
Answer: WIPS monitors the wireless network for unauthorized devices, rogue access points, and potential security threats, providing proactive security measures.

Q.304 How can you configure a wireless network to support both 2.4 GHz and 5 GHz frequency bands?
Answer: Dual-band capable access points can be configured to broadcast on both 2.4 GHz and 5 GHz bands simultaneously, providing flexibility and optimizing network performance.

Q.305 Explain the process of configuring Wireless Distribution System (WDS) for extended wireless coverage.
Answer: WDS allows interconnection between access points wirelessly. To configure it, set up WDS links between access points, ensuring they use the same security settings and SSID.

Q.306 What is the purpose of configuring a Radius server in wireless network authentication?
Answer: A RADIUS (Remote Authentication Dial-In User Service) server provides centralized authentication for wireless clients, enhancing security by validating user credentials.

Q.307 How can you troubleshoot connectivity issues in a wireless network?
Answer: Troubleshooting involves checking signal strength, analyzing interference, verifying security settings, and using tools like ping and traceroute to identify and resolve issues.

Q.308 What is the role of Quality of Service (QoS) in wireless network configuration?
Answer: QoS prioritizes certain types of traffic, ensuring that critical applications receive preferential treatment for better performance in a wireless network.

Q.309 Explain the concept of Wi-Fi Protected Setup (WPS) in wireless networks.

Answer: WPS simplifies the process of connecting devices to a secure wireless network by allowing users to press a button or enter a PIN for quick and easy configuration.

Q.310 How does firmware upgrading contribute to the security of a wireless network?

Answer: Regularly updating the firmware on wireless devices ensures that known vulnerabilities are patched, improving overall security and performance.

Q.311 What are the considerations for setting up a secure BYOD (Bring Your Own Device) policy in a wireless network?

Answer: Considerations include implementing strong authentication, isolating guest networks, monitoring and controlling device access, and educating users on security best practices.

Q.312 How can you protect against deauthentication attacks in a wireless network?

Answer: Measures against deauthentication attacks include using strong encryption (WPA3), implementing MAC filtering, and regularly monitoring for unusual activity.

Q.313 Explain the role of a wireless site survey in configuring a wireless network.

Answer: A site survey analyzes the physical environment to optimize access point placement, minimize interference, and ensure comprehensive coverage in a wireless network.

Q.314 What are the best practices for securing a wireless network against evolving threats?

Answer: Best practices include using the latest encryption standards, regularly updating firmware, monitoring network activity, implementing strong authentication, and conducting periodic security audits.

Q.315 What are the common reasons for wireless connectivity issues?

Answer: Common issues include signal interference, misconfigurations, incorrect security settings, outdated firmware, and physical obstructions.

Q.316 How can you determine the signal strength of a wireless connection?

Answer: Signal strength can be assessed using tools like Wi-Fi analyzers or by checking the signal indicator on devices. Higher signal strength indicates better connectivity.

Q.317 What steps would you take to troubleshoot a client unable to connect to a wireless network?

Answer: Steps include checking the SSID, verifying security settings, confirming the client's MAC address is allowed, and ensuring the correct wireless passphrase or key is used.

Q.318 How does channel interference impact wireless connectivity, and how can it be mitigated?

Answer: Channel interference can degrade performance. Mitigation involves selecting less crowded channels, using 5 GHz bands, and minimizing interference sources.

Q.319 Explain the role of a site survey in troubleshooting wireless connectivity.
Answer: A site survey helps identify coverage gaps, interference sources, and optimal access point placement, aiding in troubleshooting and improving overall connectivity.

Q.320 What is the significance of checking for firmware updates in wireless troubleshooting?
Answer: Firmware updates often include bug fixes and security patches that can address connectivity issues. Regular updates can improve device performance and stability.

Q.321 How can you identify and mitigate potential security threats in a wireless network?
Answer: Regularly monitor for unauthorized access, use strong encryption methods, implement MAC filtering, and conduct periodic security audits to identify and address potential threats.

Q.322 Explain the steps involved in troubleshooting slow wireless speeds.
Answer: Steps include checking signal strength, evaluating interference sources, verifying network configuration, and assessing the number of connected devices.

Q.323 What is the role of ping and traceroute in troubleshooting wireless connectivity?
Answer: Ping helps check connectivity to a specific host, while traceroute identifies the route packets take to reach the destination, aiding in diagnosing network issues.

Q.324 How can you troubleshoot intermittent wireless connectivity problems?
Answer: Troubleshooting intermittent issues involves checking for interference sources, verifying power settings, assessing signal strength, and investigating potential device or driver issues.

Q.325 What are common causes of wireless packet loss, and how can it be mitigated?
Answer: Causes include interference, high network traffic, and device issues. Mitigation involves optimizing channel selection, updating firmware, and addressing interference sources.

Q.326 How would you troubleshoot a situation where devices connect but cannot access the internet in a wireless network?
Answer: Steps include checking the router's internet connection, verifying DNS settings, ensuring proper gateway configuration, and examining firewall settings.

Q.327 What is the purpose of checking for physical obstructions when troubleshooting wireless connectivity?

Answer: Physical obstructions like walls or metal objects can attenuate wireless signals. Identifying and removing obstructions can improve signal strength and connectivity.

Q.328 How can you troubleshoot issues related to roaming in a wireless network?
Answer: Troubleshooting roaming issues involves checking for overlapping coverage areas, ensuring consistent signal strength, and verifying that devices seamlessly transition between access points.

Q.329 Explain the concept of interference from non-Wi-Fi devices in wireless troubleshooting.
Answer: Non-Wi-Fi devices, such as microwaves or cordless phones, can cause interference. Identifying and minimizing these sources can enhance wireless connectivity.

Q.330 What role does the Quality of Service (QoS) play in troubleshooting voice or video quality issues on a wireless network?
Answer: QoS prioritizes voice and video traffic, ensuring better performance. Troubleshooting involves verifying QoS settings, assessing network congestion, and optimizing bandwidth allocation.

Q.331 How can you troubleshoot a situation where some devices connect, but others do not, in a wireless network?
Answer: Troubleshooting involves checking MAC filtering settings, verifying DHCP configurations, and assessing signal strength and interference for the affected devices.

Q.332 What steps would you take to troubleshoot a wireless network that experiences frequent disconnections?
Answer: Steps include checking for interference, updating device drivers, evaluating power settings, and ensuring the wireless network is stable and properly configured.

Q.333 Explain the role of protocol analyzers or packet sniffers in wireless troubleshooting.
Answer: Protocol analyzers help capture and analyze network traffic, providing insights into packet-level details and aiding in identifying the root cause of connectivity issues.

Q.334 How can you troubleshoot a wireless network that suddenly stops working altogether?
Answer: Troubleshooting involves checking power and connectivity of devices, verifying network configurations, assessing for interference, and reviewing recent changes to identify the cause of the sudden outage.

Q.335 What is a Wide Area Network (WAN), and how does it differ from a Local Area Network (LAN)?
Answer: A WAN is a network that spans a large geographical area, connecting LANs. Unlike LANs, WANs cover a broader territory, often involving different cities or countries.

Q.336 What are the primary advantages of using WANs in networking?

Answer: WANs enable long-distance communication, facilitate resource sharing between remote locations, and support collaboration among geographically dispersed users.

Q.337 Differentiate between circuit-switched and packet-switched WAN technologies.

Answer: Circuit-switched networks establish a dedicated path for the entire duration of a communication, while packet-switched networks transmit data in discrete packets, allowing shared use of network resources.

Q.338 What is the significance of Point-to-Point Protocol (PPP) in WAN connectivity?

Answer: PPP is a data link protocol used for establishing a direct connection between two nodes over a serial link. It provides authentication, error detection, and compression capabilities.

Q.339 How does High-Level Data Link Control (HDLC) function in WAN environments?

Answer: HDLC is a bit-oriented protocol used for communication over point-to-point and multipoint links. It ensures reliable and synchronous communication between devices.

Q.340 What is Frame Relay, and what advantages does it offer in WANs?

Answer: Frame Relay is a packet-switched WAN technology that efficiently transmits data in variable-length frames. It provides cost-effective and scalable connectivity for connecting multiple locations.

Q.341 Explain the concept of leased lines in WAN connectivity.

Answer: Leased lines are dedicated, point-to-point connections between two locations. They provide a constant, always-on connection, typically used for reliable and private communication.

Q.342 What is the role of a WAN router in network architecture?

Answer: A WAN router connects local networks to wide area networks, facilitating data exchange between geographically dispersed locations. It manages traffic, enforces security policies, and optimizes data transmission.

Q.343 How does MPLS (Multiprotocol Label Switching) enhance WAN performance?

Answer: MPLS improves WAN performance by efficiently routing data based on labels, allowing for faster and more predictable data transmission compared to traditional routing methods.

Q.344 What are the key considerations in choosing between leased lines and packet-switched networks for WAN connectivity?

Answer: Leased lines offer dedicated and reliable connections but can be costlier. Packet-switched networks, like Frame Relay or MPLS, provide more flexibility and cost efficiency but may have variable performance.

Q.345 What is the purpose of WAN optimization, and how is it achieved?

Answer: WAN optimization enhances the performance of data transmission over wide area networks. Techniques include data compression, caching, and protocol optimization to minimize latency and improve efficiency.

Q.346 How does a Virtual Private Network (VPN) contribute to secure WAN communication?

Answer: VPNs use encryption and tunneling protocols to create secure, private connections over public networks. They ensure data confidentiality and integrity in WAN communication.

Q.347 Explain the concept of Quality of Service (QoS) in WANs.

Answer: QoS is a set of technologies that prioritize and manage network traffic, ensuring that critical applications receive the necessary bandwidth and low latency for optimal performance.

Q.348 What is the role of WAN accelerators in network optimization?

Answer: WAN accelerators improve data transfer speeds by employing techniques like data deduplication and compression. They optimize bandwidth utilization and enhance overall WAN performance.

Q.349 How does the Border Gateway Protocol (BGP) contribute to routing in WAN environments?

Answer: BGP is an exterior gateway protocol used for routing between different autonomous systems (AS). It enables dynamic route selection and helps routers make informed decisions for efficient data transmission.

Q.350 What is the significance of Dynamic Multipoint VPN (DMVPN) in WAN connectivity?

Answer: DMVPN is a scalable and efficient VPN solution that allows secure communication between multiple sites without requiring a direct physical connection between them.

Chapter 8: Interview Questions & Answers Part 8

Q.351 How do WAN technologies address latency challenges in long-distance communication?
Answer: WAN technologies employ optimization techniques, such as protocol acceleration and caching, to mitigate latency issues and enhance the responsiveness of applications.

Q.352 Explain the concept of a WAN cloud and its advantages.
Answer: A WAN cloud refers to a virtualized network infrastructure that provides on-demand WAN services. It offers flexibility, scalability, and cost-effectiveness for connecting remote locations.

Q.353 What are the security considerations when implementing WAN technologies?
Answer: Security measures include encryption for data in transit, secure VPN implementations, access control mechanisms, and regular monitoring for suspicious activities to protect WAN communication.

Q.354 How can WAN redundancy be implemented to ensure high availability?
Answer: WAN redundancy involves deploying multiple connections or paths between locations to ensure continuous connectivity. Techniques like link aggregation and failover mechanisms contribute to high availability.

Q.355 What is Point-to-Point Protocol (PPP)?
Answer: PPP is a data link protocol used to establish a direct connection between two network nodes, typically over a serial link, providing a reliable and efficient method for data transmission.

Q.356 What are the key features of PPP?
Answer: PPP offers features such as encapsulation, authentication, error detection, and the ability to establish point-to-point connections over various physical mediums like serial cables and telephone lines.

Q.357 How does PPP encapsulate data for transmission?
Answer: PPP encapsulates data by adding a header and trailer to the original frame, allowing for the reliable transmission of information over the network.

Q.358 What is the purpose of the PPP frame header?
Answer: The PPP frame header contains control information, including the type of data encapsulated, protocol information, and error control mechanisms.

Q.359 How does PPP handle error detection?
Answer: PPP uses a Frame Check Sequence (FCS) as part of the frame trailer for error detection. If errors are detected during transmission, the frame is discarded and retransmitted.

Q.360 Explain the role of the Link Control Protocol (LCP) in PPP.

Answer: LCP is responsible for establishing, configuring, maintaining, and terminating PPP connections. It negotiates options and parameters for the link between two PPP devices.

Q.361 What is the purpose of the Authentication phase in PPP?

Answer: The Authentication phase involves the verification of the identity of the two PPP devices. Common authentication protocols used in PPP include PAP (Password Authentication Protocol) and CHAP (Challenge Handshake Authentication Protocol).

Q.362 How does PAP differ from CHAP in PPP authentication?

Answer: PAP sends the username and password in plaintext, while CHAP uses a challenge-response mechanism, enhancing security by avoiding the transmission of passwords in clear text.

Q.363 What are the two main phases of PPP connection establishment?

Answer: The two main phases are the Link Establishment phase, where LCP negotiates parameters and options, and the Authentication phase, where the identity of the devices is verified.

Q.364 How does PPP handle network layer protocols like IP?

Answer: PPP can encapsulate various network layer protocols, such as IP, by using the Network Control Protocol (NCP). NCP is responsible for negotiating and configuring the network layer protocol.

Q.365 What is Multilink PPP (MLPPP), and why is it used?

Answer: MLPPP is an extension of PPP that allows the aggregation of multiple physical links into a single logical link. It is used to increase bandwidth and enhance reliability.

Q.366 Explain the concept of PPPoE.

Answer:PPPoE (Point-to-Point Protocol over Ethernet) is a protocol that allows PPP frames to be encapsulated within Ethernet frames, often used in broadband DSL connections.

Q.367 How does PPP handle the negotiation of options during link establishment?

Answer: LCP (Link Control Protocol) negotiates options by exchanging Configuration Request and Configuration Acknowledgment frames, allowing devices to agree on parameters for the link.

Q.368 What role does the Magic Number play in PPP?

Answer: The Magic Number is a value exchanged during LCP negotiation. It helps detect loops and ensures that the received frames match the expected values.

Q.369 How does PPP address the issue of varying link qualities?

Answer: PPP adjusts link parameters dynamically based on the quality of the connection. For example, it can negotiate different compression algorithms or adjust the frame size for optimal performance.

Q.370 What is the Maximum Transmission Unit (MTU) in the context of PPP?

Answer: MTU is the maximum size of a data frame that can be transmitted over the PPP link without fragmentation. LCP negotiation helps determine the appropriate MTU for the connection.

Q.371 How does PPP handle the termination of a connection?

Answer: LCP is responsible for terminating a PPP connection. It sends a Terminate Request frame, and upon receiving a Terminate Acknowledgment, the connection is gracefully terminated.

Q.372 Can PPP be used for both synchronous and asynchronous communication?

Answer: Yes, PPP is versatile and supports both synchronous and asynchronous communication, making it suitable for various types of physical connections.

Q.373 Explain the concept of PPP Callback.

Answer: PPP Callback is a feature that allows a PPP server to disconnect a client and call it back at a predefined number. This adds an additional layer of security and helps control costs.

Q.374 What is the primary advantage of using PPP over other protocols for point-to-point communication?

Answer: PPP is advantageous due to its flexibility, support for multiple network layer protocols, authentication mechanisms, error detection, and the ability to work over various physical mediums, making it a versatile and widely adopted protocol for point-to-point connections.

Q.375 What is Frame Relay?

Answer: Frame Relay is a packet-switched WAN technology that operates at the Data Link layer (Layer 2) of the OSI model. It provides efficient and cost-effective communication over a wide area network.

Q.376 How does Frame Relay differ from circuit-switched technologies?

Answer: Frame Relay is packet-switched, allowing multiple virtual circuits to share the same physical link simultaneously, whereas circuit-switched technologies establish a dedicated path for the entire duration of communication.

Q.377 What is a Virtual Circuit (VC) in Frame Relay?

Answer: A Virtual Circuit in Frame Relay is a logical connection established between two devices across the network. It provides a communication path for data transmission.

Q.378 Explain the concept of a Data Link Connection Identifier (DLCI) in Frame Relay.

Answer: DLCI is a numerical identifier assigned to each Virtual Circuit in Frame Relay. It is used to distinguish between different connections on the same physical link.

Q.379 What are the two types of connections in Frame Relay, and how do they differ?

Answer: The two types are Permanent Virtual Circuits (PVCs) and Switched Virtual Circuits (SVCs). PVCs are pre-configured, while SVCs are established on-demand.

Q.380 How does Frame Relay handle addressing?

Answer: Frame Relay uses DLCIs to address Virtual Circuits. It doesn't have its own addressing scheme like IP; instead, it relies on the network layer protocols, such as IP, for addressing.

Q.381 What is the significance of the Local Management Interface (LMI) in Frame Relay?

Answer: LMI is a signaling protocol used between the Frame Relay devices to exchange control information, such as status and error messages, and to manage Virtual Circuits.

Q.382 What is Frame Relay encapsulation?

Answer: Frame Relay encapsulation is the process of adding Frame Relay headers to network layer packets, allowing them to be transmitted over a Frame Relay network.

Q.383 How does Frame Relay support bandwidth conservation?

Answer: Frame Relay conserves bandwidth by using statistical multiplexing, where multiple Virtual Circuits share the same physical link based on demand.

Q.384 What is the purpose of the Committed Information Rate (CIR) in Frame Relay?

Answer: CIR is the minimum guaranteed bandwidth for a Virtual Circuit in Frame Relay. It ensures a certain level of service for the subscribed connection.

Q.385 How does Frame Relay handle error detection and correction?

Answer: Frame Relay relies on the underlying network layer protocols (e.g., IP) for error detection and correction. It does not have its own error detection mechanisms.

Q.386 What is the concept of Frame Relay encapsulation types?

Answer: Frame Relay encapsulation types define how data frames are formatted and transmitted over the physical link. The common types are Cisco, IETF, and Q933a.

Q.387 How does Frame Relay operate in a multipoint configuration?

Answer: In a multipoint configuration, a single physical link connects multiple devices. Each device has a unique DLCI, allowing communication between any two devices on the network.

Q.388 Explain the role of the Frame Relay Inverse ARP (Inverse Address Resolution Protocol).

Answer: Inverse ARP is used to map network layer addresses (such as IP addresses) to DLCIs. It dynamically discovers the mapping and simplifies the configuration of Virtual Circuits.

Q.389 What is Frame Relay fragmentation, and when does it occur?

Answer: Frame Relay fragmentation occurs when a frame is too large to fit into the Maximum Frame Size specified. The frame is then fragmented into smaller frames for transmission.

Q.390 What is the purpose of the Frame Relay Forum?

Answer: The Frame Relay Forum is an industry organization that promotes the development and interoperability of Frame Relay products. It defines standards and specifications for Frame Relay implementation.

Q.391 How does Frame Relay support network convergence?

Answer: Frame Relay allows multiple Virtual Circuits to share the same physical link, leading to efficient use of bandwidth and enabling network convergence.

Q.392 What is the role of the Data Terminal Equipment (DTE) and Data Circuit-Terminating Equipment (DCE) in Frame Relay?

Answer: DTE refers to the end-user device connecting to the Frame Relay network, while DCE refers to the network equipment (like routers) that provide the interface between the DTE and the Frame Relay network.

Q.393 Explain the concept of Frame Relay Broadcast and its implications.

Answer: Frame Relay Broadcast allows a single frame to be delivered to multiple destinations. It can lead to bandwidth utilization concerns, and some providers may charge additional fees for broadcast traffic.

Q.394 How does Frame Relay handle congestion?

Answer: Frame Relay uses mechanisms like Discard Eligibility (DE) and congestion notification to manage congestion. When congestion occurs, less critical frames may be marked as eligible for discard to prioritize essential traffic.

Q.395 What is a Virtual Private Network (VPN) in the context of Wide Area Networks (WANs)?

Answer: A VPN is a secure and private communication network established over a public or shared network infrastructure, such as the internet, to connect remote locations or users securely.

Q.396 What are the primary benefits of using VPNs in WANs?

Answer: VPNs provide secure data transmission over untrusted networks, enable cost-effective connectivity between geographically dispersed locations, and allow remote users to access the corporate network securely.

Q.397 Differentiate between Site-to-Site VPNs and Remote Access VPNs.

Answer: Site-to-Site VPNs connect entire networks or sites, while Remote Access VPNs allow individual users to connect securely to a network from remote locations.

Q.398 How does encryption contribute to the security of VPNs?

Answer: Encryption ensures that data transmitted over the VPN is protected from eavesdropping or unauthorized access. It transforms the data into a secure format that can only be deciphered with the appropriate decryption key.

Q.399 What protocols are commonly used for VPN encryption?

Answer: Common VPN encryption protocols include IPsec (Internet Protocol Security), SSL/TLS (Secure Sockets Layer/Transport Layer Security), and PPTP (Point-to-Point Tunneling Protocol).

Q.400 Explain the concept of Tunneling in VPNs.

Answer: Tunneling involves encapsulating data packets within a new set of headers to create a secure communication channel or "tunnel" between two points on a network.

Chapter 9: Interview Questions & AnswersPart 9

Q.401 How does IPsec contribute to VPN security?

Answer: IPsec provides a suite of protocols for securing internet communications. It offers authentication, integrity, and confidentiality, making it widely used in VPN implementations.

Q.402 What is the purpose of a VPN Concentrator in VPN deployments?

Answer: A VPN Concentrator is a device that aggregates multiple VPN connections. It optimizes bandwidth, manages encryption/decryption, and provides centralized control over VPN access.

Q.403 How does Split Tunneling impact VPN traffic?

Answer: Split Tunneling allows some traffic to go through the VPN tunnel, while other traffic directly accesses the internet. It can reduce VPN traffic and improve overall performance but may pose security risks.

Q.404 What is the role of a VPN Gateway in VPN architectures?

Answer: A VPN Gateway serves as an entry and exit point for VPN traffic, connecting the local network to the VPN. It manages the establishment and termination of VPN connections.

Q.405 How can Multi-Protocol Label Switching (MPLS) be integrated with VPNs?

Answer: MPLS can be used to create Virtual Private Networks (MPLS VPNs), providing a scalable and efficient method for connecting multiple locations securely.

Q.406 Explain the significance of Dynamic Multipoint VPN (DMVPN) in VPN architectures.

Answer: DMVPN is a scalable VPN solution that simplifies the establishment of VPN connections between multiple sites without requiring a direct physical connection between them.

Q.407 What is the role of a VPN Client in Remote Access VPNs?

Answer: A VPN client is software installed on a user's device that facilitates secure communication with the VPN server, allowing remote users to access the corporate network securely.

Q.408 How does SSL/TLS VPN differ from IPsec VPN?

Answer: SSL/TLS VPN operates at the application layer and is often used for remote access. IPsec VPN operates at the network layer and is commonly used for site-to-site connections.

Q.409 Explain the concept of GRE (Generic Routing Encapsulation) in VPNs.

Answer: GRE is a tunneling protocol that encapsulates a wide variety of network layer protocols inside point-to-point connections. It is often used to create VPN tunnels.

Q.410 What are the considerations for choosing between SSL and IPsec VPNs?

Answer: SSL VPNs are often preferred for remote access due to their ease of use and compatibility with web browsers. IPsec VPNs are commonly used for site-to-site connections due to their robust security features.

Q.411 How does a VPN ensure confidentiality in data transmission?
Answer: A VPN achieves confidentiality by encrypting the data during transmission. Only devices with the appropriate decryption keys can decipher and access the original information.

Q.412 What is the role of Network Address Translation (NAT) in VPN configurations?
Answer: NAT may be used to translate private IP addresses into a public address space, allowing VPN traffic to traverse the internet securely without revealing internal network details.

Q.413 How can a VPN contribute to compliance with regulatory requirements, such as data privacy laws?Answer: VPNs provide a secure and encrypted means of transmitting sensitive data, helping organizations comply with data privacy regulations by safeguarding data during transit.

Q.414 What security measures should be implemented to enhance VPN security?
Answer: Implementing strong encryption, multi-factor authentication, regular security audits, and keeping VPN software up-to-date are crucial measures for enhancing VPN security.

Q.415 What is SNMP, and what role does it play in network management?
Answer: SNMP is a protocol used for managing and monitoring network devices. It allows network administrators to retrieve information and configure devices remotely.

Q.416 Explain the three main components of SNMP.
Answer: SNMP consists of a Management Station (MS) responsible for collecting and analyzing data, Managed Devices (MDs) like routers and switches being monitored, and Agents, software on MDs that collects and sends information to the MS.

Q.417 What are the SNMP versions, and how do they differ?
Answer: SNMP has three versions: SNMPv1, SNMPv2c, and SNMPv3. SNMPv1 has limited security features, SNMPv2c enhances SNMPv1 but still lacks robust security, while SNMPv3 introduces authentication and encryption for secure communication.

Q.418 What is an SNMP community string, and why is it important?
Answer: A community string acts as a password between the SNMP manager and the SNMP agent. It is essential for authenticating and authorizing SNMP requests.

Q.419 How does SNMP use MIBs (Management Information Bases)?

Answer: MIBs define the structure and attributes of the data that can be managed using SNMP. They provide a standardized way to organize information about devices on a network.

Q.420 Explain the difference between SNMP traps and informs.

Answer: SNMP traps are unsolicited notifications sent by the agent to the manager when an event occurs. SNMP informs are similar but require acknowledgment from the manager.

Q.421 What is the purpose of Syslog in network management?

Answer: Syslog is a protocol used for collecting and forwarding log messages from network devices. It helps in monitoring, troubleshooting, and auditing network events.

Q.422 How does Syslog prioritize log messages?

Answer: Syslog uses severity levels (0 to 7) to prioritize log messages. Levels range from emergencies (0) to debugging (7), with decreasing severity.

Q.423 What are the three components of a Syslog message?

Answer: A Syslog message consists of a timestamp, hostname or IP address of the device, and the actual log message with severity and facility information.

Q.424 Explain the concept of Syslog facilities.

Answer: Syslog facilities categorize messages into different functional areas, such as kernel, user, mail, and local use. Facilities help in organizing and filtering log messages.

Q.425 How can Syslog messages be centralized in a network?

Answer: Syslog messages can be centralized using a Syslog server. Network devices send their log messages to the Syslog server, providing a centralized location for monitoring and analysis.

Q.426 What is the role of the Syslog severity level "Emergency"?

Answer: The "Emergency" severity level (level 0) indicates a system-wide crisis requiring immediate attention. It is the most critical level in Syslog.

Q.427 How does SNMP contribute to proactive network management?

Answer: SNMP enables proactive network management by allowing administrators to monitor network devices, collect performance data, and receive alerts about potential issues before they impact the network.

Q.428 What security measures can be implemented in SNMPv3 to protect against unauthorized access?

Answer: SNMPv3 provides security features like authentication and encryption. Implementing strong passwords, configuring access control, and using encryption enhance SNMPv3 security.

Q.429 What is the purpose of SNMP polling?

Answer: SNMP polling involves the manager periodically querying SNMP agents for specific information. It is used to monitor device performance and gather data for analysis.

Q.430 How does SNMPv3 address the limitations of previous SNMP versions?

Answer: SNMPv3 enhances security by introducing authentication and encryption, addressing the vulnerabilities present in SNMPv1 and SNMPv2c.

Q.431 What is a Syslog relay, and why might it be used in a network?

Answer: A Syslog relay is a device that forwards Syslog messages from one network segment to another. It is used to centralize log information from different parts of the network.

Q.432 How can SNMP traps be configured on a network device?

Answer: SNMP traps are configured on a network device by setting up the SNMP agent to send trap notifications to a specific SNMP manager when predefined events occur.

Q.433 What is the role of the Syslog severity level "Warning"?

Answer: The "Warning" severity level (level 4) indicates a potentially harmful event that should be investigated but does not require immediate attention. It is less critical than "Emergency."

Q.434 How does SNMP contribute to network fault management?

Answer: SNMP aids in network fault management by providing real-time monitoring, quick detection of device issues, and alerting administrators about faults, allowing for prompt troubleshooting and resolution.

Q.435What is the importance of troubleshooting in network management?

Answer: Troubleshooting is crucial for identifying and resolving issues in a network, ensuring optimal performance, minimizing downtime, and maintaining a reliable and secure infrastructure.

Q.436Explain the difference between reactive and proactive troubleshooting.

Answer: Reactive troubleshooting involves resolving issues as they occur, while proactive troubleshooting involves identifying and addressing potential problems before they impact the network.

Q.437What are the key steps in the troubleshooting process?

Answer: The troubleshooting process typically involves identifying the problem, establishing a theory of probable cause, testing the theory, determining the cause, implementing a solution, and verifying the solution.

Q.438How does the OSI model aid in troubleshooting network issues?

Answer: The OSI model provides a structured approach to troubleshooting by breaking down network functions into distinct layers. It helps isolate issues to specific layers and facilitates a systematic resolution approach.

Q.439Explain the concept of the "divide and conquer" strategy in troubleshooting.

Answer: The "divide and conquer" strategy involves breaking down a complex problem into smaller, more manageable parts. It helps isolate the root cause and simplifies the troubleshooting process.

Q.440What role does documentation play in troubleshooting?

Answer: Documentation is essential for recording network configurations, changes, and troubleshooting steps. It aids in tracking network history, sharing information among team members, and expediting future problem resolution.

Q.441How can network monitoring tools assist in troubleshooting?

Answer: Network monitoring tools provide real-time insights into network performance, allowing administrators to detect anomalies, identify bottlenecks, and address issues proactively.

Q.442What is the significance of establishing a baseline in troubleshooting?

Answer: Establishing a baseline involves documenting normal network behavior. It serves as a reference point for identifying deviations, enabling faster detection and resolution of abnormal conditions.

Q.443How do you approach troubleshooting a network issue when users report slow internet connectivity?

Answer: I would start by checking the network utilization, examining bandwidth usage, and identifying potential bottlenecks. Then, I would investigate individual devices, analyze configurations, and assess the overall network health.

Q.444What is the difference between a "top-down" and "bottom-up" troubleshooting approach?

Answer: In a top-down approach, you start with the end-user's experience and work downward through the layers of the OSI model. In a bottom-up approach, you begin at the physical layer and move upward.

Q.445How can the use of simulation tools aid in troubleshooting?

Answer: Simulation tools allow for the replication of network environments, enabling administrators to test configurations and troubleshoot potential issues in a controlled, risk-free environment.

Q.446What is the role of packet analysis in network troubleshooting?

Answer: Packet analysis involves examining network packets to identify anomalies, errors, or irregularities. It is valuable for diagnosing issues related to packet loss, latency, or misconfigurations.

Q.447How do you prioritize troubleshooting tasks when dealing with multiple reported issues?

Answer: Prioritization involves assessing the impact of each issue on the network and addressing critical problems first. It ensures that the most significant issues are resolved promptly.

Q.448Explain the concept of the "50-50 rule" in troubleshooting.

Answer: The "50-50 rule" suggests dividing the troubleshooting process into two parts: spend 50% of the time gathering information to understand the problem and the remaining 50% implementing a solution.

Q.449What is the role of historical data in troubleshooting recurring issues?

Answer: Historical data provides insights into patterns, trends, and recurring issues. Analyzing historical information helps identify underlying causes and implement preventive measures.

Q.450How can collaboration with other team members enhance the troubleshooting process?

Answer: Collaboration involves sharing information, expertise, and insights among team members. It accelerates problem resolution by leveraging collective knowledge and skills.

Chapter 10: Interview Questions & Answers Part 10

Q.451What steps would you take to troubleshoot intermittent network connectivity issues?

Answer: Troubleshooting intermittent issues involves checking for environmental factors, inspecting cable connections, analyzing network logs, and using diagnostic tools to capture and analyze intermittent events.

Q.452Explain the concept of "backtracking" in troubleshooting.

Answer: Backtracking involves revisiting earlier troubleshooting steps when new information becomes available or when initial assumptions prove incorrect. It helps refine the troubleshooting process based on evolving insights.

Q.453How can a systematic approach to troubleshooting benefit the network administrator?

Answer: A systematic approach ensures that no steps are skipped, reduces the likelihood of overlooking critical details, and facilitates a methodical and efficient resolution of network issues.

Q.454What role does vendor support play in the troubleshooting process?

Answer: Vendor support provides access to technical expertise, documentation, and assistance in resolving issues specific to the hardware or software involved. Collaborating with vendors can expedite problem resolution.

Q.456What are some common causes of network latency, and how can they be mitigated?

Answer: Network latency can be caused by congestion, inefficient routing, or long-distance transmissions. Mitigating measures include optimizing network paths, implementing Quality of Service (QoS), and using content delivery networks (CDNs).

Q.457How do you troubleshoot issues related to DNS resolution?

Answer: Troubleshooting DNS issues involves checking DNS server availability, verifying DNS configurations on devices, and examining domain records. Clearing DNS caches and using alternative DNS servers can also help.

Q.458 What steps would you take to resolve issues with IP address conflicts?

Answer: Resolving IP address conflicts requires identifying conflicting devices, updating IP configurations, and ensuring DHCP servers are properly configured to prevent address conflicts.

Q.459How can you diagnose and address issues related to network congestion?

Answer: Network congestion can be diagnosed by monitoring traffic patterns. Solutions include implementing QoS, optimizing network paths, and upgrading network infrastructure to handle increased traffic.

Q.460What could be the reasons for slow internet connectivity in an organization, and how would you troubleshoot it?

Answer: Slow internet connectivity may result from bandwidth limitations, ISP issues, or internal network congestion. Troubleshooting involves checking bandwidth usage, contacting the ISP, and optimizing internal network configurations.

Q.461How do you troubleshoot issues with network connectivity for a specific device?

Answer: Troubleshooting device-specific connectivity issues involves checking physical connections, verifying IP configurations, testing cabling, and using diagnostic tools like ping and traceroute.

Q.462What steps would you take to troubleshoot a network outage?

Answer: Troubleshooting a network outage includes checking device power, verifying cable connections, examining network device logs, and using diagnostic commands like ping and show commands on routers and switches.

Q.463How can you identify and address issues related to duplicate MAC addresses on a network?

Answer: Identifying duplicate MAC addresses involves checking network logs and using tools like ARP tables. Resolving the issue requires locating and isolating the devices with duplicate MAC addresses and updating configurations.

Q.464What are the common causes of packet loss, and how can it be minimized?

Answer: Packet loss can result from network congestion, hardware failures, or faulty cables. Minimizing packet loss involves optimizing network paths, replacing faulty hardware, and implementing error correction techniques.

Q.465How would you troubleshoot issues with a specific application not working over the network?

Answer: Troubleshooting application-specific issues involves checking application logs, verifying network connectivity, and ensuring that required ports are open. Examining firewall settings and contacting application vendors may also be necessary.

Q.466What could be the reasons for intermittent connectivity issues, and how would you troubleshoot them?

Answer: Intermittent connectivity issues may result from cable problems, device interference, or network congestion. Troubleshooting involves checking physical connections, inspecting cabling, and using diagnostic tools to capture intermittent events.

Q.467How do you troubleshoot issues related to DHCP failures?

Answer: Troubleshooting DHCP failures includes checking DHCP server availability, verifying DHCP configurations, and ensuring that there are no IP address conflicts. Examining logs and using diagnostic tools can help identify the root cause.

Q.468What steps would you take to troubleshoot issues with a wireless network?

Answer: Troubleshooting wireless network issues involves checking signal strength, verifying security configurations, and examining interference from other devices. Updating firmware and optimizing channel selection can improve wireless performance.

Q.469How can you identify and address issues related to a switch not forwarding traffic?

Answer: Identifying switch forwarding issues involves checking port status, examining switch logs, and using diagnostic commands like show commands on the switch. Resolving the issue may require port reconfiguration or replacement of faulty hardware.

Q.470What are the common causes of network loops, and how can they be prevented?

Answer: Network loops can be caused by Spanning Tree Protocol (STP) misconfigurations or faulty cabling. Preventive measures include configuring STP correctly, implementing loop prevention mechanisms, and using redundant links carefully.

Q.471How would you troubleshoot issues related to a router not routing traffic between subnets?

Answer: Troubleshooting router routing issues involves checking routing table entries, verifying subnet configurations, and examining routing protocols. Updating configurations, checking ACLs, and using diagnostic tools can help identify and resolve the problem.

Q.472What steps would you take to troubleshoot issues with a firewall blocking legitimate traffic?

Answer: Troubleshooting firewall issues involves checking firewall logs, examining rule configurations, and ensuring that necessary ports are open. Verifying the source and destination addresses and updating firewall rules can resolve the issue.

Q.473How can you diagnose and address issues related to VLAN configurations?

Answer: Diagnosing VLAN configuration issues involves checking switch configurations, examining VLAN assignments, and verifying trunking configurations. Resolving the issue may require updating VLAN assignments and checking trunk configurations.

Q.474What could be the reasons for network performance degradation, and how would you address it?

Answer: Network performance degradation may result from increased traffic, hardware limitations, or inefficient configurations. Addressing it involves optimizing network paths, upgrading hardware, and implementing QoS mechanisms.

Q.475How do you troubleshoot issues related to a network printer not responding?

Answer: Troubleshooting network printer issues involves checking printer connectivity, verifying IP configurations, and examining print queues. Updating printer drivers, checking for paper or toner issues, and ensuring proper power supply can resolve the problem.

Q.476What steps would you take to troubleshoot issues with a router losing connectivity to the internet?
Answer: Troubleshooting router connectivity issues involves checking WAN interface configurations, verifying ISP connectivity, and examining routing tables. Resolving the issue may require updating IP configurations, checking ISP connections, and using diagnostic tools.

Q.477How can you identify and address issues related to a network device not receiving power?
Answer: Identifying power issues involves checking power cables, verifying power outlets, and examining device power indicators. Resolving the issue may require replacing faulty power cables, ensuring proper power sources, and replacing defective power supplies.

Q.478What could be the reasons for issues with a network server not responding to requests?
Answer: Server responsiveness issues may result from high server loads, software failures, or network connectivity problems. Troubleshooting involves checking server logs, examining resource utilization, and verifying network connectivity.

Q.479How would you troubleshoot issues with a router or switch console port not responding?
Answer: Troubleshooting console port issues involves checking physical connections, verifying console port configurations, and examining device logs. Resolving the issue may require updating configurations, replacing faulty cables, or using alternative console ports.

Q.480What steps would you take to troubleshoot issues with a network device experiencing high CPU utilization?
Answer: Troubleshooting high CPU utilization involves checking device logs, examining running processes, and identifying resource-intensive applications. Resolving the issue may require updating device firmware, optimizing configurations, and implementing traffic filtering.

Q.481How can you identify and address issues related to a network cable not providing a stable connection?
Answer: Identifying cable issues involves checking cable connectors, verifying cable integrity, and using cable testers to identify faults. Resolving the issue may require replacing faulty cables, ensuring proper termination, and avoiding cable interference.

Q.482 What are the common causes of broadcast storms, and how can they be prevented?

Answer: Broadcast storms can be caused by network loops, faulty network interfaces, or excessive broadcast traffic. Preventive measures include implementing Spanning Tree Protocol (STP), monitoring network traffic, and optimizing broadcast domains.

Q.483How would you troubleshoot issues with a network device not obtaining an IP address from DHCP?
Answer: Troubleshooting DHCP issues involves checking DHCP server availability, verifying DHCP configurations, and examining device logs. Resolving the issue may require updating DHCP configurations, checking DHCP server availability, and using diagnostic tools.

Q.484What steps would you take to troubleshoot issues with a network device experiencing intermittent disconnections?
Answer: Troubleshooting intermittent disconnections involves checking physical connections, verifying device configurations, and examining network logs. Resolving the issue may require updating configurations, replacing faulty hardware, or addressing interference.

Q.485How can you identify and address issues related to a network device not recognizing other devices on the same subnet?
Answer: Identifying recognition issues involves checking device configurations, verifying subnet settings, and examining ARP tables. Resolving the issue may require updating configurations, checking subnet settings, and using diagnostic tools.

Q.486What is the significance of using network troubleshooting tools in network management?
Answer: Network troubleshooting tools are essential for diagnosing and resolving network issues efficiently. They provide insights into network performance, help identify faults, and aid administrators in maintaining a healthy network.

Q.487 Name some common network troubleshooting tools and their purposes.
Answer: Common network troubleshooting tools include Ping (testing connectivity), Traceroute (identifying network path), nslookup (DNS resolution), Wireshark (packet analysis), and ipconfig/ifconfig (viewing IP configurations).

Q.488 How does the Ping tool work, and what information does it provide?
Answer: Ping sends ICMP Echo Request messages to a target device and measures the round-trip time for a response. It helps test network connectivity and provides information about packet loss and latency.

Q.489 Explain the purpose of the Traceroute tool.

Answer: Traceroute traces the route that packets take from the source to the destination. It helps identify the number of hops, delays, and potential issues along the network path.

Q.490 How can the nslookup tool assist in network troubleshooting?

Answer:nslookup is used to query DNS servers for domain-related information. It helps troubleshoot DNS issues by verifying domain name resolutions and querying specific DNS records.

Q.491 What is the role of Wireshark in network troubleshooting?

Answer: Wireshark is a packet analyzer that captures and analyzes network traffic. It helps identify network anomalies, diagnose protocol issues, and troubleshoot performance problems.

Q.492 How does the ipconfig/ifconfig tool aid in troubleshooting network connectivity?

Answer: ipconfig (Windows) and ifconfig (Unix/Linux) display IP configuration details for a device. They help troubleshoot connectivity issues by providing information about IP addresses, subnet masks, and gateway settings.

Q.493 What is the purpose of the netstat tool in network troubleshooting?

Answer: netstat displays network statistics and active connections. It aids in troubleshooting by showing open ports, active connections, and routing information on a device.

Q.494 Explain the role of the Telnet tool in network troubleshooting.

Answer: Telnet is used to establish a connection to a remote device over a network. It helps troubleshoot connectivity issues by verifying if a specific port is open and responsive.

Q.495 How does the ARP (Address Resolution Protocol) tool assist in network troubleshooting?

Answer: ARP resolves IP addresses to MAC addresses on a local network. The ARP tool helps troubleshoot connectivity issues by displaying and managing ARP tables.

Q.496 What is the purpose of the PathPing tool, and how does it differ from Ping?

Answer: PathPing combines features of Ping and Traceroute. It tests connectivity to a destination like Ping but provides Traceroute-like information about the network path taken by packets.

Q.497 How can the iperf tool be useful in network troubleshooting?

Answer:iperf measures network bandwidth between two devices. It is useful for troubleshooting by assessing network performance, identifying bottlenecks, and optimizing bandwidth usage.

Q.498 Explain the role of the Nmap tool in network troubleshooting.

Answer: Nmap is a network scanning tool that helps identify open ports, services, and potential vulnerabilities on a network. It is useful for security and troubleshooting purposes.

Q.499 What is the purpose of the SNMP (Simple Network Management Protocol) tool?

Answer: SNMP is a protocol for managing and monitoring network devices. SNMP tools assist in troubleshooting by allowing administrators to retrieve information and configure devices remotely.

Q.500 How does the TFTP (Trivial File Transfer Protocol) tool contribute to network troubleshooting?

Answer: TFTP is used for simple file transfers. In troubleshooting, it helps transfer configuration files, firmware updates, or logs between devices on a network.

Chapter 11: Interview Questions & Answers Part 11

Q.501 What is the role of the Packet Capture feature in network troubleshooting tools like Wireshark?
Answer: Packet Capture captures and records network traffic for analysis. It is valuable in troubleshooting by providing a detailed view of packet-level information for diagnosing issues.

Q.502 How can a cable tester be useful in network troubleshooting?
Answer: A cable tester helps identify faulty cables, miswiring, or connectivity issues in network cables. It aids in diagnosing physical layer problems in the network.

Q.503 What is the purpose of the PRTG Network Monitor tool?
Answer: PRTG Network Monitor is used for real-time monitoring of network devices, bandwidth usage, and performance metrics. It aids in troubleshooting by providing insights into network health.

Q.504 Explain the significance of the Path Computation Element Communication Protocol (PCEP) in network troubleshooting.
Answer: PCEP is used to communicate between a Path Computation Element (PCE) and a Path Computation Client (PCC) in network environments. It assists in troubleshooting by optimizing and computing network paths dynamically.

Q.505 How does the NetFlow tool contribute to network troubleshooting?
Answer: NetFlow is a network protocol that provides visibility into network traffic by collecting and analyzing flow data. It helps in troubleshooting by identifying sources of congestion, monitoring bandwidth usage, and detecting anomalies.

Q.506 What is the purpose of the iperf3 tool, and how does it differ from the original iperf?
Answer: iperf3 is an updated version of iperf that supports multiple streams for better accuracy in measuring network bandwidth. It is used to assess network performance and troubleshoot bandwidth-related issues.

Q.507 How can the Cisco IOS Embedded Event Manager (EEM) assist in network troubleshooting?
Answer: EEM is a scripting tool in Cisco devices that allows the automation of tasks based on events. It aids in network troubleshooting by automating responses to specific events, alerts, or issues.

Q.508 Explain the role of the SmokePing tool in network troubleshooting.
Answer: SmokePing measures network latency and packet loss over time. It is used to troubleshoot by providing graphical representations of network performance and identifying trends or patterns.

Q.509 What is the purpose of the Netcat tool in network troubleshooting?

Answer: Netcat is a versatile networking utility that can be used for various tasks, including port scanning, file transfers, and network testing. In troubleshooting, it assists in establishing connections and sending/receiving data.

Q.510 How does the Cisco Packet Tracer tool aid in network troubleshooting?

Answer: Cisco Packet Tracer is a simulation tool for Cisco networks. It helps in troubleshooting by allowing users to simulate and test network configurations, addressing issues in a virtual environment.

Q.511 What is the purpose of the Remote Desktop Protocol (RDP) in network troubleshooting?

Answer: RDP allows users to connect to remote desktops. In troubleshooting, it enables administrators to remotely access and troubleshoot issues on devices without physical presence.

Q.512 Explain the role of the Cisco CLI Analyzer tool in network troubleshooting.

Answer: Cisco CLI Analyzer is a cloud-based tool that assists in analyzing Cisco CLI commands. It helps troubleshoot by providing recommendations, command syntax checks, and historical command analysis.

Q.513 How can the Nagios tool be beneficial in network troubleshooting?

Answer: Nagios is an open-source monitoring tool that provides alerts and reports on network and system issues. It aids in troubleshooting by detecting and notifying administrators about potential problems.

Q.514 What is the purpose of the ipmitool in network troubleshooting?

Answer:ipmitool is used to manage hardware through Intelligent Platform Management Interface (IPMI). It assists in troubleshooting by providing remote management capabilities for devices like servers.

Q.515 How does the Cisco Network Assistant tool contribute to network troubleshooting?

Answer: Cisco Network Assistant is a graphical network management tool for Cisco devices. It aids in troubleshooting by providing a user-friendly interface for configuring, monitoring, and diagnosing network issues.

Q.516What is Routing?

Answer: Routing is the process of finding a path on which data can pass from source to destination. Routing is done by a device called routers, which are network layer devices

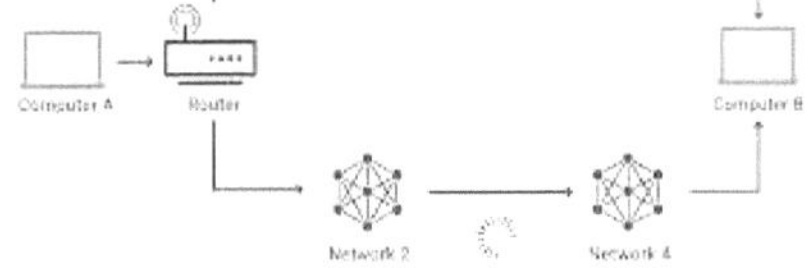

Q.517 What is the purpose of the Data Link?

Answer: The job of the Data Link layer is to check messages are sent to the right device. Another function of this layer is framing.

Q.518 What is the key advantage of using switches?

Answer: When a switch receives a signal, it creates a frame out of the bits that were from that signal. With this process, it gains access and reads the destination address, after which it forwards that frame to the appropriate port. This is a very efficient means of data transmission, instead of broadcasting it on all ports.

Q.519 When does network congestion occur?

Answer: Network congestion occurs when too many users are trying to use the same bandwidth. This is especially true in big networks that do not resort to network segmentation.

Q.520 What is a Window in networking terms?

Answer: A Window refers to the number of segments that are allowed to be sent from source to destination before an acknowledgment is sent back.

Q.521 Does a bridge divide a network into smaller sections?

Answer: Not really. What a bridge actually does is to take the large network and filter it, without changing the size of the network.

Q.522 Which LAN switching method is used in CISCO Catalyst 5000?

Answer: CISCO Catalyst 5000 uses the Store-and-forward switching method. It stores the entire frame to its buffers and performs a CRC check before deciding whether or not to forward that data frame.

Q.523 What is the role of the LLC sublayer?

Answer: The LLC sublayer stands for Logical Link Control. It can provide optional services to an application developer. One option is to provide flow control to the Network layer by using stop/start codes. The LLC can also provide error correction.

Q.524 How does RIP differ from IGRP?

Answer: RIP relies on the number of hops in order to determine the best route to a network. On the other hand, IGRP takes consideration many factors before it decides the best route to take, such as bandwidth, reliability, MTU and hop count.

Q.525 What are the different memories used in a CISCO router?

Answer: Different memories used in a CISCO router are:

– NVRAM stores the startup configuration file.

– DRAM stores the configuration file that is being executed.

– Flash Memory – stores the Cisco IOS.

Q.526 What is BootP?

Answer: BootP is a protocol that is used to boot diskless workstations that are connected to the network. It is short for Boot Program. Diskless workstations also use BootP in order to determine its own IP address as well as the IP address of the server PC.

Q.527 What is the function of the Application Layer in networking?

Answer: The Application Layer supports the communication components of an application and provides network services to application processes that span beyond the OSI reference model specifications. It also synchronizes applications on the server and client.

Q.528 Differentiate User Mode from Privileged Mode.

Answer: User Mode is used for regular task when using a CISCO router, such as to view system information, connecting to remote devices, and checking the status of the router. On the other hand, privileged mode includes all options that are available for User Mode, plus more. You can use this mode in order to make configurations on the router, including making tests and debugging.

Q.529 What is 100BaseFX?

Answer: This is Ethernet that makes use of fiber optic cable as the main transmission medium. The 100 stands for 100Mbps, which is the data speed.

Q.530 Differentiate full-duplex from half-duplex.

Answer: In full-duplex, both the transmitting device and the receiving device can communicate simultaneously, that is, both can be transmitting and receiving at the same time. In the case of half-duplex, a device cannot receive while it is transmitting, and vice versa.

Q.531 What is MTU?

Answer: MTU stands for Maximum Transmission Unit. It refers to the maximum packet size that can be sent out onto the data line without the need to fragment it.

Q.532 How does cut-through LAN switching work?

Answer: In Cut-Through LAN switching, as soon as the router receives the data frame, it will immediately send it out again and forward it to the next network segment after reading the destination address.

Q.533 What is latency?

Answer: Latency is the amount of time delay that measures the point from which a network device receives a data frame to the time it sends it out again towards another network segment.

Q.534 Utilizing RIP, what is the limit when it comes to the number of hops?

Answer: The maximum limit is 15 hop counts. Anything higher than 15 indicates that the network is considered unreachable.

Q.535 What is a Frame Relay?

Answer: Frame Relay is a WAN protocol that provides connection-oriented communication by creating and maintaining virtual circuits. It has a high-performance rating and operates at the Data Link and Physical Layers.

Q.536 How do you configure a Cisco router to route IPX?

Answer: The initial thing to do is to enable IPX routing by using the "IPX routing" command. Each interface that is used in the IPX network is then configured with a network number and encapsulation method.

Q.537What are the different IPX access lists?

Answer: There are two types of IPX access lists

1. Standard.

2. Extended.

Standard Access List can only filter the source or destination IP address. An Extended Access List uses the source and destination IP addresses, port, socket, and protocol when filtering a network.

Q.538 Explain the benefits of VLANs.

Answer: VLANs allow the creation of collision domains by groups other than just physical location. Using VLANs, it is possible to establish networks by different means, such as by function, type of hardware, protocol, among others. This is a big advantage when compared to conventional LANs wherein collision domains are always tied to physical location.

Q.539 What is subnetting?

Answer: Subnetting is the process of creating smaller networks from a big parent network. As a part of a network, each subnet is assigned some additional parameters or identifier to indicate its subnet number.

Q.540 What are the advantages of a layered model in the networking industry?

Answer: A layered network offers many advantages. It allows administrators to make changes in one layer without the need to make changes in the other layers. Specialization is encouraged, allowing the network industry to make progress faster. A layered model also lets administrators troubleshoot problems more efficiently.

Q.541 Why is UDP lease favored when compared to TCP?

Answer: It's because UDP is unreliable and unsequenced. It is not capable of establishing virtual circuits and acknowledgments.

Q.542 What are some standards supported by the Presentation layer?

Answer: Presentation layer supports many standards, which ensures that data is presented correctly. These include PICT, TIFF, and JPEG for graphics, MIDI, MPEG and QuickTime for Video/Audio.

Q.543 What's the easiest way to remotely configure a router?

Answer: In cases when you need to configure a router remotely, the most convenient is to use the Cisco AutoInstall Procedure. However, the router must be connected to the WAN or LAN through one of the interfaces.

Q.544 What does the show protocol display?

Answer:

– routed protocols that is configured on the router.

– the address assigned on each interface.

– the encapsulation method that was configured on each interface.

Q.545 How do you depict an IP address?

Answer: It can be done in three possible ways:

– using Dotted-decimal. For example: 192.168.0.1

– using Binary. For example: 10000010.00111011.01110010.01110011

– using Hexadecimal. For example: 82 1E 10 A1

Q.546 How do you go to privileged mode? How do you switch back to user mode?

Answer: To access privileged mode, you enter the command "enable" on the prompt. In order to get back to user mode, enter the command "disable."

Q.547What is HDLC?

Answer: HDLC stands for High-Level Data Link Control protocol. It is a propriety protocol of CISCO. It is the default encapsulation operated within CISCO routers.

Q.548 How are internetworks created?

Answer: Internetworks are created when networks are connected using routers. Specifically, the network administrator assigns a logical address to every network that connects to the router.

Q.549 What is Bandwidth?

Answer: Bandwidth refers to the transmission capacity of a medium. It is a measure of how much volume a transmission channel can handle, and it is measured in Kbps.

Q.550How does Hold-downs work?

Answer: Hold-downs prevent regular update messages from reinstating a downed link by removing that link from update messages. It uses triggered updates to reset the hold-down timer.

Chapter 12: Interview Questions & AnswersPart 12

Q.551 What are packets?

Answer: Packets are the results of data encapsulation. These are data that have been wrapped under the different protocols of the OSI layers. Packets are also referred to as datagrams.

Q.552 What are segments?

Answer: Segments are sections of a data stream that comes from the upper OSI layers and ready for transmission towards the network. Segments are the logic units at the Transport Layer.

Q.553 Give some benefits of LAN switching.

Answer:

– allows full duplex data transmission and reception

– media rate adaption

– easy and efficient migration

Q.554 What is Route Poisoning?

Answer: Route Poisoning is the process of inserting a table entry of 16 to a route, making it unreachable. This technique is used in order to prevent problems caused by inconsistent updates on a route.

Q.555 How do you find valid hosts in a subnet?

Answer: The best way to go about this is to use the equation 256 minus the subnet mask. The hosts that are considered valid are those that can be found between the subnets.

Q.556 What is DLCI?

Answer: DLCI, or Data Link Connection Identifiers, are normally assigned by a frame relay service provider in order to uniquely identify each virtual circuit that exists on the network.

Q.557 Briefly explain the conversion steps in data encapsulation.

Answer: From a data transmitter's point of reference, data from the end user is converted to segments. Segments are then passed on to the other layers and converted into packets or datagrams. These packets are then converted into frames before passing on to the network interface. Finally, frames are converted to bits prior to actual data transmission.

Q.558 What are the different types of passwords used in securing a CISCO router?

Answer: There are actually five types of passwords that can be used. These enable secret, virtual terminal, console, and auxiliary.

Q.559 Why is network segmentation a good idea when managing a large network?

Answer: For a network administration, segmenting a network would help ease network traffic and ensures that high bandwidth is made available at all times for all users. This translates to better performance, especially for a growing network.

Q.560 What are the things that can be accessed in a CISCO router's identifying information?

Answer: The hostname and the Interfaces. The hostname is the name of your router. The Interfaces are fixed configurations that refer to the router ports.

Q.561Differentiate Logical Topology from Physical Topology

Answer: Logical Topology refers to the signal path through the physical topology. Physical Topology is the actual layout of the network medium.

Q.562 What causes a triggered update to reset the router hold-down timer?

Answer: This may happen when the hold-down timer has already expired, or when the router received a processing task that incidentally was proportional to the number of links in the internetwork.

Q.563What is the difference between the switch, hub, and router?

Answer:

Hub: Hub has a single broadcast domain and collision domain. Anything comes in one port is sent out to the others.

Switch: It is a device that filters and forwards packets between LAN segments. Switches have a single broadcast domain and multiple collision domains. It supports any packet protocol, as such it operates at the data link layer 2 and layer 3

Router: Router is a device which transmits data packets along networks.

Q.564Mention what does data packets consist of?

Answer: A data packet consists of sender's information, recipient's information, and the data contained. It also has the numeric identification number that defines the packet number and order. When data is sent across the network, that information is segmented into data packets. In short, data packets carry the information and routing configuration for your transferred message.

Q.565What is DHCP stand for?

Answer: DHCP stands for Dynamic Host Configuration Protocol. DHCP assigns an IP address automatically to a given workstation client. You can also make static IPS for machines like printers, servers, routers, and scanners.

Q.566Mention what BOOTP is?

Answer: BOOTP is a computer networking protocol used to deploy an IP address to network devices from a configuration server.

Q.567 Explain why UDP is lease favored when compared to TCP?

Answer: It is because UDP is un-sequenced and unreliable. It is not capable of creating virtual circuits and acknowledgments.

Q.568 State the difference between dynamic IP and static IP addressing?

Answer: Dynamically IP addresses are provided by DHCP server, and static IP addresses are given manually.

Q.569 What is EIGRP?

Answer: EIGRP stands for Enhanced Interior Gateway Routing Protocol it is a routing protocol designed by Cisco Systems. It is availed on a router to share routes with other routers within the same autonomous system. Unlike other routers like RIP, EIGRP only sends incremental updates, decreasing the workload on the router and the amount of data that needs to be transferred.

Q.570 Mention what command you must use if you want to delete or remove the configuration data that is stored in the NVRAM?

Answer: Erase startup- coding is the command you must use if you want to delete the configuration data that is stored in the NVRAM.

Q.571 What is the difference between TCP and UDP?

Answer: TCP (Transmission Control Protocol), UDP (User Datagram Protocol)TCP is connection oriented protocol. When connection lost during transferring files, the server would request the lost part. While transferring a message, there is no corruption while transferring a message UDP is based on connectionless protocol. When you send data, there is no guarantee whether your transferred message will reach there without any leakage. The message will deliver in the order it is sent. The message you sent may not be in the same orderData in TCP is read as a stream, where one packet ends, and another begins. Packets are transmitted individually and are guaranteed to be whole if they arrive. Example of TCP includes World Wide Web, file transfer protocol, e-mail, Example for UDP are VOIP (Voice Over Internet Protocol) TFTP (Trivial File Transfer Protocol).

Q.572 Explain the difference between half-duplex and full-duplex?

Answer: Full duplex means that the communication can occur in both directions at the same time, while half-duplex means that the communication can happen in one direction at a time.

Q.573 What route entry will be assigned to dead or invalid route in case of RIP?

Answer: In the case of RIP table entry, 16 hops will be assigned to dead or invalid route making it unreachable.

Q.574 Explain OSI Layer?

Answer:

1. Open system interconnect (OSI) was developed by the international organization for standardization (ISO) and introduced in 1984.

2. It's a consists of seven layers.

3. Application layer, Presentation layer, Session layer, Transport layer, Network layer, Data link layer, Physical layer.

Q.575 What are Different protocol works at each of the Layer in OSI model?

Answer:

Application layer: It's responsible for providing an interface for the user to interact with application services or network services.

Ex-Web browser (HTTP), Telnet.

Presentation layer: It's responsible for defining a standard format to the data. The major functions described at this layer are: - Encoding-Decoding.

Ex- AVI-(video), WAV-(voice), JPEG (graphite), ASCII (text) Encryption-Decryption.

Session layer: It's responsible for establishing, maintaining, and terminating the sessions. Session ID is used to identify a session or interaction.

Ex-Remote procedural call, Apple talk session protocol

Transport Layer: It provides data delivery mechanism between applications in the network. Transport layer is the major function layer In OSI layer Identifying service Multiplexing & De-multiplexing Segmentation, Error correction, flow control Transport layer protocols? The protocols which take care of data transport at transport layer are TCP/UDP.

Q.576 What is the key advantage of using switches?

Answer: When a switch receives a signal, it creates a frame out of the bits that were from that signal. With this process, it gains access and reads the destination address, after which it forwards that frame to the appropriate port. This is a very efficient means of data transmission, instead of broadcasting it on all ports.

Q.577 What is a Window in networking terms?

Answer: A Window refers to the number of segments that are allowed to be sent from source to destination before an acknowledgment is sent back.

Q.578 Does a bridge divide a network into smaller sections?

Answer: Not really. What a bridge actually does is to take the large network and filter it, without changing the size of the network.

Q.579 Which LAN switching method is used in CISCO Catalyst 5000?

Answer: CISCO Catalyst 5000 uses the Store-and-forward switching method. It stores the entire frame to its buffers and performs a CRC check before deciding whether or not to forward that data frame.

Q.580 What is the function of a MAC address?

Answer: A MAC address is a unique identifier assigned to a network interface card (NIC) that allows devices to communicate with each other on a network.

Q.581 What is the function of a subnet mask?

Answer: A subnet mask is used to divide a network into smaller subnetworks, allowing for more efficient routing and network management.

Q.582 What is the function of DHCP?

Answer: DHCP (Dynamic Host Configuration Protocol) is a protocol used to automatically assign IP addresses and other network configuration settings to devices on a network.

Q.583 What is the difference between static and dynamic routing?

Answer: Static routing involves manually configuring routes on each router, while dynamic routing allows routers to automatically discover and update routes based on information received from other routers.

Q.584 What is the purpose of NAT (Network Address Translation)?

Answer: NAT is used to translate private IP addresses to public IP addresses, allowing devices on a private network to access the Internet.

Q.585 What is the function of a firewall?

Answer: A firewall is a network security device that monitors and controls incoming and outgoing network traffic based on a set of security rules.

Q.586 What is the difference between HTTP and HTTPS?

Answer: HTTP (Hypertext Transfer Protocol) is an unencrypted protocol used for transferring data between web browsers and web servers, while HTTPS (Hypertext Transfer Protocol Secure) is an encrypted version of HTTP that provides secure communication.

Q587 What is the purpose of DNS (Domain Name System)?

Answer: DNS is a hierarchical naming system used to translate human-readable domain names (e.g., www.example.com) into IP addresses, which are used by computers to locate and communicate with each other on the Internet.

Q.588 What is the function of a proxy server?

Answer: A proxy server acts as an intermediary between a client and a server, providing various services such as caching, security, and filtering of network traffic.

Q.589 What is the difference between IPv4 and IPv6?

Answer: IPv4 (Internet Protocol version 4) is the current version of the Internet Protocol, while IPv6 is the next-generation IP addressing system designed to address the limitations of IPv4, such as the limited number of available IP addresses.

Q.590 What is the purpose of a VPN (Virtual Private Network)?

Answer: A VPN allows users to securely access a private network over a public network, such as the Internet.

Q.591 What is the function of a load balancer?

Answer: A load balancer distributes incoming network traffic across multiple servers, improving performance and reliability.

Q.592 What is the purpose of a repeater?

Answer: A repeater is a networking device that amplifies and retransmits signals, extending the reach of a network.

Q.593 What is the function of a bridge?

Answer: A bridge is a networking device that connects two or more LANs (Local Area Networks), allowing devices on different LANs to communicate with each other.

Q.594 What is the difference between a client and a server?

Answer: A client is a device that requests and consumes data or services from a server, while a server is a device that provides data or services to clients.

Q.595 What is the purpose of a network operating system (NOS)?

Answer: A NOS is an operating system designed specifically for managing and controlling a computer network.

Q.596 What is the function of a file server?

Answer: A file server is a computer dedicated to storing and managing files, allowing multiple users to access and share files over a network.

Q.597 What is the difference between a firewall and an intrusion detection system (IDS)?

Answer: A firewall prevents unauthorized access to a network, while an IDS detects and responds to security breaches and attacks.

Q.598 What is the purpose of a network management system (NMS)?

Answer: An NMS is a software application used to monitor and manage network devices and resources.

Q.599 What is the function of a network protocol analyzer?

Answer: A network protocol analyzer is a tool used to capture and analyze network traffic for troubleshooting and security purposes.

Q.600 What is the difference between a WAN and a LAN?

Answer: A WAN (Wide Area Network) connects devices and networks over a large geographical area, while a LAN (Local Area Network) connects devices and networks within a limited physical space, such as a building or campus.

Q.601 What is the purpose of a modem?

Answer: A modem modulates and demodulates signals, allowing computers and other devices to communicate over analog telephone lines.

Q.602 What is the function of a router?

Answer: A router is a networking device that connects multiple networks and determines the best path for data to travel.

Q.603 What is the difference between a static IP address and a dynamic IP address?

Answer: A static IP address is a permanent IP address assigned to a device, while a dynamic IP address is assigned temporarily and can change over time.

Q.604 What is the purpose of a DNS server?

Answer: A DNS server translates domain names into IP addresses, allowing devices to locate and communicate with each other on the Internet.

Q.605 What is the function of a web server?

Answer: A web server is a computer that stores and delivers web pages and other web content to clients.

Q.606 What is the difference between a web browser and a search engine?

Answer: A web browser is a software application used to access and view web pages, while a search engine is a tool used to find information on the Internet.

Q.607 What is the purpose of an email server?

Answer: An email server is a computer that stores, sends, and receives email messages.

Q.608 What is the function of a VPN client?

Answer: A VPN client is a software application that allows a device to connect to a VPN server and create a secure connection over a public network.

Q.609 What is the default gateway in a network?

Answer: The default gateway is the router that serves as the exit point for data packets leaving a LAN. It forwards packets to their intended destination networks.

Q.610 What is the function of a DHCP server?

Answer: A DHCP (Dynamic Host Configuration Protocol) server automatically assigns IP addresses and other network configuration parameters to devices on a network, simplifying network management and reducing the risk of IP address conflicts.

Q.611 What is NAT (Network Address Translation)?

Answer: NAT is a technique used to translate private IP addresses used within a network to public IP addresses for accessing the internet, allowing multiple devices to share a single public IP address.

Q.612 What is the purpose of a firewall?

Answer: A firewall is a network security device that monitors and controls incoming and outgoing network traffic, blocking unauthorized access and protecting the network from security threats.

Q.613 What is the difference between a LAN and a WAN?

Answer: A LAN (Local Area Network) is a network that connects devices within a limited physical area, such as a building or campus, while a WAN (Wide Area Network) connects devices over a larger geographic area, such as a city or country.

Q.614 What is the function of a VPN (Virtual Private Network)?

Answer: A VPN creates a secure encrypted tunnel over a public network, allowing remote users to securely access private networks as if they were physically connected.

Q.615 What is the purpose of QoS (Quality of Service)?

Answer: QoS is a set of techniques used to prioritize and manage network traffic, ensuring that critical applications and data receive the necessary bandwidth and performance.

Q.616 What is the purpose of a proxy server?

Answer: A proxy server acts as an intermediary between a client and a server, handling requests and responses on behalf of the client, improving performance, security, and anonymity.

Q.617 What is the difference between a fiber optic cable and a copper cable?

Answer: Fiber optic cables use light pulses to transmit data, while copper cables use electrical signals. Fiber optic cables offer higher bandwidth, lower latency, and greater security compared to copper cables.

Q.618 What is the purpose of a network protocol?

Answer: A network protocol is a set of rules and procedures that govern how devices communicate with each other on a network. Common network protocols include TCP/IP, HTTP, and FTP.

Q.619 What is the function of a network interface card (NIC)?

Answer: A NIC is a hardware component that connects a device to a network. It provides the physical connection and handles data transmission and reception.

Q.620 What is the difference between a modem and a router?

Answer: A modem is a device that modulates and demodulates signals, allowing devices to communicate over telephone lines or cable lines. A router is a device that connects multiple networks and forwards data packets between them.

Q.621 What is the purpose of a network address translation (NAT) device?

Answer: A NAT device translates private IP addresses used within a network to public IP addresses for accessing the internet, allowing multiple devices to share a single public IP address.

Q.622 What is the function of a virtual private network(VPN)?

Answer: A VPN creates a secure encrypted tunnel over a public network, allowing remote users to securely access private networks as if they were physically connected.

Q.623 What is the difference between a network operating system (NOS) and a general-purpose operating system (GPOS)?

Answer: A NOS is an operating system specifically designed for managing and controlling network resources, while a GPOS is a general-purpose operating system designed for running applications on a computer.

Q.624 What is the purpose of a domain name system (DNS) server?

Answer: A DNS server translates human-readable domain names (e.g., www.example.com) into machine-readable IP addresses, enabling devices to communicate with each other across the internet.

Q.625 What is the function of a switch?

Answer: A switch is a networking device that connects multiple devices together and forwards data packets between them. It operates at Layer 2 of the OSI model and uses MAC addresses to determine where to forward data packets.

Q.626 What is the difference between a router and a bridge?

Answer: A router connects multiple networks together and forwards data packets between them based on their IP addresses. A bridge connects two or more LAN segments together and forwards data packets between them based on their MAC addresses.

Q.627 What is the difference between a virtual LAN (VLAN) and a physical LAN (PLAN)?

Answer: A VLAN is a logical LAN created within a physical LAN, allowing devices on the same VLAN to communicate with each other as if they were on the same physical LAN, even if they are physically located on different parts of the network. A PLAN is a physical.

Q.628 What is the difference between a network switch and a router?

Answer: A network switch operates at Layer 2 of the OSI model and connects devices within the same LAN, while a router operates at Layer 3 and connects different networks by forwarding data packets based on their IP addresses.

Q.629 What is the purpose of a Spanning Tree Protocol (STP)?

Answer: STP is a protocol used to prevent loops in a network. It ensures that there is only one active path between any two devices on a network, preventing unnecessary traffic andimproving network performance.

Q.630 What is the difference between a unicast, multicast, and broadcast transmission?

Answer: Unicast transmission is a one-to-one communication where data is sent from a single source to a single destination. Multicast transmission is a one-to-many communication where data is sent from a single source to multiple destinations. Broadcast transmission is a one-to-all communication where data is sent from a single source to all devices on a network.

Online Resources:

Practice Paper :https://forms.gle/YqoN4fcJSNrJ3GXv5

QR Code :

Video Link: https://youtu.be/yT6ChhKyaQw?si=0-L6HbuOaDuuLAdq

QR Code :

Additional Resources

YouTube: https://youtu.be/IqQAc9Wi6wU

Exam URL: https://forms.office.com/r/MYfBCuz5r8?origin=lprLink

Exam QR Code: